y's Dedication

rtain that Jesus lived and gave his life for the redemption of
at we may know God and live a life bound by the principles
and grace. My faith in these Christian principles defines my
nd my ability to live life according to God's will. Everything
ntemplate in life is based on the teaching of Jesus Christ.
this, I dedicate this work to Christ Jesus and His Church.

this would have been possible without my dad. Tom
is a man who has dedicated his entire life to his children.
ng soul has given me more than anyone could ever give. He
to the golf course. He has loved me unconditionally
ut my life. No matter what the circumstances, pleasant or
nt, he has never wavered. He is the most reliable person I
always gave me the security to know that everything was
st fine.

g mother, Sandra, whose life ended too soon, but supplied
nending love and support; it was my mother who instilled
faith. Her comforting words, "Son I will be praying for
e resounded in my mind every day since she left us.

Mary Hamrick were my father's parents. It is without
hat they are two individuals who have forever left an
on my heart that is everlasting. My grandmother, Joyce
ho has played golf her whole life, has measured me with
nal love and care since I have been alive. I am so thankful

w much God loves us because that is how much I love
n, Mary Clay and Mason. Everything that I do in life is
am so very blessed to have such wonderful children. Life
mpossible without them. I dedicate this work to them. I
d of them, and I hope I bring them as much pleasure as
me. They are what my life and times are all about.

MW01097745

Life Lessons from the Golf Course:
The Quest for Spiritual Meaning, Psychological Understanding and Inner Peace through the Game of Golf

By Clay Hamrick, PGA Professional

With Don McNay, CLU, ChFC, MSFS, CSSC
Best-selling author, syndicated columnist, structured settlement
consultant

RRP International LLC

Don's granddaughter, Adelaide Bigler, preparing for the 2032 Pro Tour

Don's Dedication

"Forgive me, Lord, if sometimes I forget
You know about the reasons that are hid
You understand the things that gall or fret
Well, you knew me better than my mother did"
-Johnny Cash

It was Clay Hamrick's calling to focus on my health and physical conditioning and teach me to truly enjoy playing golf.

It was my calling to get Clay's message to the world.

The book is obviously dedicated to Clay. He is a loyal and insightful friend, an intensely devoted father, a deep thinker and a man I trust to teach my children and grandchildren about golf and life. Behind his intense exterior is the heart of a lion.

It is also dedicated to the people who helped me reconnect with the power of prayer and took me from a hospital bed to Clay's golf course.

Karen Thomas McNay, Anne Parton, Crystal Martin Hamblin, Sydney Napier Thigpen and Nicole Gilliam were the people who made it happen.

My late father was a professional gambler. If you made a bet that my road to spiritual and physical redemption would include a golf pro, school principal, hair stylist, office professional and a couple of nurses, he would have calculated odds higher than winning the lottery.

This proves that the Lord works in mysterious ways. And unlikely ways as well.

I thank God for bringing those people into my life and dedicate this book to them.

Table of Contents

Introduction by Don McNay..9

I. Understanding Consciousness..................................17

II. Peace of Mind...29

III. Overcoming the Ego..37

IV. Spiritual Accomplishment....................................44

V. Simplicity...56

VI. Respect Not Fear...66

VII. The Mind and the Self...77

VIII. Pressure...83

IX. Redemption...94

X. Transcendence..100

Clay's Acknowledgments...108

Don's Acknowledgments..113

About Clay Hamrick...116

About Don McNay..118

Don (left) golfing with friends, including Boston Red Sox star Fred Lynn (middle), in San Diego 2004

Introduction

"Talk to God and listen to his casual reply"
-John Denver

"Faith is taking the first step even when you don't see the whole staircase."
- Dr. Martin Luther King, Jr.

"I'm going to give you a little advice. There's a force in the universe that makes things happen. And all you have to do is get in touch with it, stop thinking, let things happen and be the ball."
-Ty Webb (Chevy Chase) in the movie *Caddyshack*

My road back to golf and to Clay Hamrick was a spiritual one.

December 2011 caused me to face my two biggest fears: surgery in general and prostate surgery in particular.

My father died a painful death from prostate cancer at age 59. Since his death in 1993, I have been a fanatic about taking the PSA exam and being examined for prostate cancer. I've fought with doctors and insurance companies. I insist on being tested far more than insurance company guidelines.

When I started having intense pain in the prostate region, I kept on going. When I started stopping every 15 to 20 minutes to use the bathroom, I kept on going. I figured that with all of my testing and worry, prostate cancer could not happen to me. Also, I did not want to find out it could.

By December, I was in such pain that I couldn't drive. I still insisted on taping a weekly segment I was doing for a local television station. By fluke or divine intervention, the person I asked to drive me to the station, Anne Parton, was new to my organization, but had trained to be a registered nurse.

Anne insisted on driving me to the emergency room, where the doctors drained 17 pounds of fluid from my bladder. I was lucky to be alive. After a couple of weeks of unsuccessful treatment options, I had to face my next biggest fear: surgery.

I help people who receive large sums of money, and I'm an expert in a field called structured settlements. Although I am best known for my work with lottery winners, the vast majority of my clients are injury victims and many of the big cases come from medical malpractice.

I've seen people go in for routine surgery and die. I've seen others come out in wheelchairs. I had one client go in for minor knee surgery and come out with a heart transplant. It took a major league screw-up to have that happen. Although statistically the overwhelming majority of people who have surgery come out fine, I've spent 30 years with the ones who don't.

I made it from age five to age 52 without being in a hospital. For anything. Suddenly, I did not have a choice.

Then, I did something I had not done in a long time. I prayed. And got an army of people, mostly from my Facebook page, of different faiths, religions and spiritual beliefs to pray along with me.

I came to the conclusion that one of two things could happen: I would live or die and go to heaven.

The thought gave me the peace and the courage to face the surgery.

Which did not go well.

Karen Thomas, my fiancé at the time (and now my wife), is now the president of the Ursuline Academy in New Orleans, the oldest Catholic school in the United States, but at the time was principal of Christ the King Elementary in Lexington.

Although I have 12 years of Catholic education and served as president of my church council, I had fallen away from organized religion several years ago.

Being in a potential life or death situation changed that tune immediately.

On the day of my surgery, Karen took me to see a priest to hear my confession and give me last rites in case something went wrong.

Something did go wrong. Because of a scheduling screw-up, I was prepped for surgery and waited for eight hours, only to be told to come back two days later.

I kept hoping I did not commit any sins during the two days, but since I was in screaming, intense pain, I did not have much opportunity.

On the second try, the hospital staff fell over themselves to make up for the mistake, and I was the first person taken to surgery. I woke up a few hours later, attached to my now-familiar catheter. I had a very rough night, which included a bad experience with an unpleasant and inexperienced nurse.

Getting into it with the nurse was a traumatic experience.

I love nurses. My late mother was an operating room nurse for 27 years, and my family and friends endowed the Ollie McNay nursing scholarship at Eastern Kentucky University after her death.

It's impossible for me to not see my mother in every nurse I encounter. I treat them with the respect that mom deserved and didn't always get.

After that horrible night, I tried to call and email my family and friends to get me out of the place. It was very early in the morning, and I couldn't find anyone.

Then, the shift changed and my guardian angel arrived.

In the movie *It's a Wonderful Life*, George Bailey (played by Jimmy Stewart) had a guardian angel who was an older, prissy man named Clarence.

My guardian angel was a mid-20s nurse assistant from Nicholasville, Ky., named Crystal Hamblin.

Once Crystal and the registered nurse she worked with, Sydney Napier Thigpen, came on the scene, life got better.

Crystal is now a massage therapist, and at the time she only worked in the hospital every other weekend. Fortunately, she was scheduled for my weekend.

Crystal is street smart with tons of common sense. She is a source of calm, but she was dealing with a middle-age man who wanted to jump out of his skin.

She and I immediately became (and remain) friends, and she walked me through some deep breathing exercises. She changed my gown, helped me get out of bed and made me feel human again.

The message hit me that little things are what life is all about.

Sydney and I hit it off right away, too. Syd has the work ethic and concern for her patients that reminded me of my mom. Because of a blood clot and other issues, it looked like I may have to be operated on again, but Crystal and Sydney were my angels. Along with the power of prayer, they kept me calm.

They found a resident and a bunch of other nurses, and with several intense efforts, they broke the blood clot.

A few days later, the urologist told me I did not have cancer. I was in horrible pain and missed out on Christmas and New Year's, but I had plenty of reasons to celebrate.
My present was the outpouring of love, prayers and support, many from people who only read about me on Facebook.

Just like George Bailey, I've lived a wonderful life and had not always appreciated it.

Having so many people praying reminded me that prayer is a universal language. I connected with angels at the hospital, but I also connected with the angels up above.

Prayer had been missing from my life for years, and I was reminded of why it is a tenet of every faith in the world.

Having everything happen during the Christmas season gave me time to deeply reflect.

When my father had a stroke at age 43, he prayed for three things. He prayed that he would live long enough to see a grandchild, and my nephew Nick came into the world a few years later. He prayed that he would meet the right life partner, and he hit the jackpot with my stepmother Lynn. He wanted one of his children to graduate from college, and I made that prayer happen.

Based on my father's model, I prayed for similar life events. One that I articulated was I wanted to play golf again. I had stopped about a decade earlier as I decided I was too fat to play. I was not in the physical condition to play nine holes.

Going through surgery made me determined to take better care of myself. And to find an instructor who could get me excited about playing golf again.

I feel like God's hand led me to Clay Hamrick.

Clay came from an unlikely referral source. We both use the same stylist, Nicole Gilliam. Clay has a full head of perfectly styled hair, and it takes Nicole about five minutes to trim my few remaining locks.
The odds of both of us using the same hairdresser are improbable. However, I told Nicole I was looking for a golf instructor, and she

gave me Clay's number.

Our hair style is not the only difference between Clay and me. We are different ages, with different body sizes and distinctly different political views. However, we immediately became close friends.

Clay is well-educated and extremely well-read. Like myself, he is an intense competitor and has an incredible work ethic.

He is one of the best golf teachers I have ever encountered, especially with young children. Unlike most instructors, he is not just a student of the game, but a student of life and all the things that make us do what we do.

Golf is not about striking a ball with a club. It is about all those things in our psychological makeup that allow us to play the game to the best or worst of our abilities.

When a professional golfer misses a short putt and loses a major championship, it was not lack of training that caused the ball to be mishit; it was something in the core of their inner self.

Clay understands this. It did not surprise me when he said he had been working on a book for a number of years. It surprised me when he said it was a golf instruction book.

I wasn't all that excited about reading his manuscript. As I told him at the time, the world doesn't need another book about how to keep your elbows straight. I've read all of them, and they just made my game worse.

He is my friend, so I took it home to read anyway.

I was stunned at what he had written. I started reading it in the parking lot of his golf course and could not put it down. I called him at home that night to arrange dinner the next day.
I told him that his book was not about golf, it was about psychology and spirituality. Golf was just the mechanism to advance his theories

and thoughts.

I asked to be his co-author and help him organize the book into 10 chapters, like the Ten Commandments, and coach him in his writing the way that he has coached me in golf.

He agreed.

I've taken 80 golf lessons with Clay, and thanks to his instruction and coaching, at age 54 I play the best golf of my life. Being on the course brings me a sense of inner peace, fun and accomplishment that I have never felt in a sports environment before.

When you read *Life Lessons from the Golf Course*, you will be touched by Clay's tremendous insights and passion, but you will see how the skills he is teaching translate to every aspect of life.

Golf is a microcosm of life. This book is a chance to learn about golf, but also learn about being in touch with yourself and with a higher power.

The power of prayer got me to Clay Hamrick.

This book will be the answer to many people's prayers. It will make them better golfers, but also better people.

I'm proud to be part of making that happen.

Don McNay

Marshall Pickett and Clay Hamrick Homecoming: A successful Qualifying School adventure

I. Understanding Consciousness

"If you bring forth what is within you, what you bring forth will save you. If you do not bring forth what is within you, what you do not bring forth will destroy you."
-Jesus Christ

Great teaching begins with great information and an open mind. Great coaching starts with great players. Teaching and coaching are indeed different. This is why it is so important to study our thoughts and feelings. Our thoughts and feelings provide a blueprint for successful growth even though we are all different thinkers and feelers. We all can probe into our self or ego to understand the conscious material that helped develop our unconscious, which causes unintended actions, thoughts and feelings.

The exploration of the unconscious is complex, but the unconscious itself is simple. Getting to repressed material may be difficult to accomplish, but understanding the unconscious should not be. The unconscious is very honest. It knows what hurts and helps, and it holds feelings until the body or consciousness allows it to be useful or makes us sick. The conscious mind can also be destructive or helpful. It can be simple by nature, but it brings about a great deal of confusion and complexity if not used constructively. It is where the ego lives.

Sigmund Freud was the inventor of the Psychoanalytic Theory. Freud was a smart man, but also seemed a bit eccentric. He did some excellent work in defining psychological terminology and had a profound interest in philosophy.

The Psychoanalytic Theory that Freud exposed deals strictly with repressed information that has been hidden in the unconscious. But psychoanalysis proves unnecessary if a patient has an open and honest reflection about thoughts, feelings and life experiences. People are much healthier when willing to admit problems, analyze what went right or wrong and then move on with confidence and clarity. Psychoanalysis does prove useful in situations where repressed feelings are unknown to the patient. If that is the case, psychoanalysis can be a very useful practice.

However, individuals usually are a victim of their own points of view more so than the unknown, unconscious experience. We become bound by our own point of view more than our circumstances or past experience.

Much of what we think and feel is not derived from our unconscious. The unconscious is simple-minded. The unconscious makes us understand black and white, not much gray. It knows what works for us and what does not. It logs feelings that have manifested over time.

If we are about to hit a golf ball, we must understand the objective. The unconscious knows what the objective is. It is to hit the ball, nothing else. The game is simple! It is our consciousness that gets in the way of true performance. If the golf swing lacks fundamental structure, the unconscious is still going to hit the ball in some direction because that is the objective. It maintains a sense of accomplishment because it hit the ball. The conscious mind feeds wrong information to the brain and makes us react to the physical programming.

So many people act like swing thoughts are the root of all evil. Swing thoughts can be damaging because most of us think thoughts that produce negativity. If our swing is not working, it has to be a problem with the mechanics. What else could it be? The unconscious leads us to hitting. In this case, the unconscious is the caveman. It is non-intellectual and quite infantile. It knows that the hitting will be inefficient if the swing lacks sound mechanical process. The brain already knows what it takes to hit the ball efficiently.

Take my eight-year-old son. He is very young, but yet he hits the ball time after time in the middle of the face. I can pretend that he is an intellectual prodigy with an ability to understand the mechanical process of the golf swing, but that would be silly. He has just figured out that he has to rip the club inside, keep his weight steady and finish his swing. He has perfect balance and an ability to do it over and over again. So why can he hit the ball and I can't? I have toyed with my swing so much that my conscious mind has been polluted with bad information.

How do I overcome this? My mind could be getting in the way. I would rather think that the programming my mind was telling my body was faulty with dysfunctional information that lacked structure. My mind was creating a mess.

The mind is an interesting thing. It works hand in hand with our body. That is why people exercise. The reason many people exercise is because they are looking for psychological/emotional reinforcement rather than physical fitness. Think about the weightlifter who looks in the mirror after every set on the bench press, or the person who is always in the front row of the aerobics class. These people are looking for psychological satisfaction more than physical fitness.

Every infomercial on television talks about the emotional and psychological aspect of getting in shape instead of our basic health needs. The physical process that we go through in any exercise will always do as much for our minds as it does for our bodies. That is why our organic mixture is always connected to our psychological health. We already have thoughts and feelings locked deep within our unconscious that we carry around. We also have material that we act upon, but never make known to our conscious mind.

Think of all the physical and mental processes we need to drive a car. If we knew that we had to do all these things on a conscious level, there would be five times the car accidents there already are. We even talk on phones and listen to music and radio while we drive. The reason we can do everything we do while we drive is because we have an unconscious comfort with our physical activity. We know how to move our arms and legs in tandem and move the steering wheel because those activities are physically sound movements that are functional.

Imagine if your golf swing was physically functional. Your balance was perfect, your plane angles and club face agreed with the flight pattern of the ball. You would have total control of your ball flight and your power. The unconscious is now thinking for you because your physical swing works. This is a new referendum for all teaching. So how do we get to unconscious golf?

Some think we come to a state of golfing prowess from a Darwinian frame work of natural selection. Some have it, some don't, the environment chooses. I would like to think that we actually learn what we are doing and perform what we have learned. I prefer learning, because it is never fleeting. It means we always have an understanding of what we can accomplish with the proper amount of practice.

I am reminded of a junior golfer years ago in California who was thought to be a child prodigy. He knew nothing about his swing, but he was a very functional ball striker. After securing a tour card years later in his young adult life, he felt he needed to learn as much about his swing as he could in order to stay at the top of his game. The problem was that he plugged in bad information. He only knew of one way to swing and that was unconsciously etched in his brain.

He re-learned a new swing. He changed everything, and lo and behold, he could not play. He could not understand why. He had a functional swing and did not realize it. He then plugged in bad information that his unconscious knew would not work and struggled.

The disagreement between mind and body led to things like the deterioration of his mental confidence. This guy knew he could not play. He hit the ball short and right. It fed into his putting and chipping. Eventually, he quit the pro tour and had to re-learn everything he did as a child, but this time he proved it scientifically. He then structured the information in a way that could be studied. He eventually regained his tour card and had a successful career.

We have spent time focusing on the good player, but what about the average, everyday player? How do they get their two minds working together? First of all, we have to go back to the idea of learning the proper mechanics that can help relieve the mind and body's disagreement. Proper mechanics can be learned on any level.

Remember, having too much thought is not necessarily bad, especially if the thought leads to learning. Information is looked upon as a burden in golf. It must be acted upon and used as a metric for results. The conscious mind has to process this information and understand it. For an amateur, structure and practice are more important because of talent, experience and unconscious programming. Good players are good because they know it and feel like they can accomplish their goals because they have done it over and over. Their unconscious mind is programmed to help the body act with balance, feel, timing and rhythm, creating a very nice golf game.

Amateurs need to understand that knowledge is power. They may not have the early programming needed to grow into a world championship golf player, so they need to compensate with a cognitive conscious learning process. I think Tiger Woods would have been great had he started playing golf when he was 16. But his early programming occurred when he did not have the luxury or burden of an analytic mind. Children just do not have that brain crystallization, meaning analytic development, necessary to analyze information. The younger we learn something, the more it can stick with us because our brain is not analytic; it just absorbs the information.

For those who do not start early, they must understand the brain has now developed into a machine that needs information. What is put into the brain is crucial, just like what we put into our bodies. We do what we think we understand, and we swing how we think it should feel.

The most confusing data in sports history is golf instruction. An even bigger source of confusion is incomplete information like golf tips, which are very small pieces of information dealing with easy adjustments. I myself have been a victim of golf tips that have worked. But the tips were always fleeting. Nothing ever stuck because there was no point of reference.

Structure is essential in maintaining something great over a long period of time. We must ask why do our swing and game leave us, and what role do our two minds, unconscious and conscious, play in that process? The conscious part of our mind is responsible for cognition or thinking. Here we derive what we think to be important and worthy of our recognition. Our unconscious houses all the unrealized information that we are not aware of most of the time, but is carried with us at all times.

Our cognition has to be used like a computer. It must have the information put in, evaluated and learned. That information has to resonate with the person and, in this case, be transferred to the physical body in the vehicle of a golf swing. The golfer loses his swing because of nothing other than his point of reference. If a golfer takes a lesson and learns the basics of the grip, the lesson must be rehearsed over and over again until the nervous system learns what the cognition has entered. If the grip becomes a problem, it is because the reference point has not been noticed consciously.

After our conscious process has been practiced, all the neurotic behaviors (or anxieties) begin. Basic anxieties such as nervousness, impatience, irrational thinking and fear are just a few identifiable neuroses. Much of this unwanted material is born in the unconscious and then triggered when fear and insecurity are recognized consciously. Our cognition is responsible for the creation of fear and insecurity by unnecessary amounts of self-talk, situational fears or reactions to environment. Either way, we have to deal with these neurotic tendencies in order to achieve the outcomes that we want.

Before beginning to outline the problematic areas of conscious anxiety and unconscious repression, we must understand that all people have neurotic tendencies. Some handle these insecurities better than others and that is what makes a difference in performance. Some individuals will develop confidence that is reinforced very early in life. Children who tend to be confident are reinforced by events and people such as parents, grandparents and friends. These individuals are not aware of any other circumstance. They feel comfortable with themselves, which makes it easier for them to perform.

Those who have struggled with confidence have to become more of a student. They have not been reinforced by their results; therefore, they learn to combat anxiety more effectively through other vehicles such as physical training, information or counseling. They have to use their cognition more in order to reinforce the idea that they can do it. But can they totally eliminate unconscious fear and the triggers that produce unwanted responses? That is the million dollar question.

Have you ever stood on the first tee and wondered how you were going to take the club back and hit the ball? You were so nervous and tight that it just seemed impossible to make your swing. Why does this happen? The conscious mind is the shallowest form of consciousness. It judges our environment through observation and then ignites the self-talk that can create unwanted feelings and emotions. The unconscious is the "file server." It stores all the information we have compiled about ourselves and what has happened in our environment. We can be aware of our self, but our self is active to our conscious.

Our comfort zone is created in our unconscious. But can our conscious thoughts interfere with our comfort? Absolutely! If given the opportunity, we can talk ourselves into or out of just about anything. When approaching an environment that creates anxiety, we know that our unconscious has been made aware of a situation where we are not comfortable. Our responses are defined by actions, emotions or feelings. For example, someone who is very insecure with their ability is always trying to update their résumé or explain their case in front of other people. After we are confronted with these responses, we then begin to self-talk through our consciousness. These feelings can be positive or negative, depending on the unconscious picture we draw of ourselves.

When we are in an uncomfortable environment and are used to internal turmoil, we are more likely to deal with things like "first tee jitters" better than those who have never been placed in that situation. Some may never recognize the uncomfortable nature of that particular environment and welcome the challenge of the big shot. That is truly a blessing. These are the folks that want the ball at the end of the game or go for the green when everything is on the line. If they fail, it is of no consequence to their psyche. They just do. The doers are usually the ones with the best psychological outlook.

Others who are not comfortable in the environment always look for ways out of that very difficult situation. They are quick to hit or take an extreme amount of time. Very rarely can they get through their routine without experiencing anxiety. They are the excuse makers. They only do these things because they are afraid and do not feel good about what they are doing.

A tour player I watched not too long ago is a terrific player who took the lead of the US Open into the final round. He is a long hitter, has great hands and can be an exceptional putter. He had never led a major championship before going into the final round. When I saw him come to the tee on the final day, I could see something was not quite right. He seemed different. He proceeded to hit a poor tee shot off the first and made a triple bogey. He faded from the leader board quickly and has not played well in the majors since.

What was happening inside the mind of this player? I certainly do not know. But he was not ready to win the US Open. Of course, no one is ever ready to win or lose anything, and many people win in life just because others lose. But why did he play his worst game on the last day when he finally had the lead?

Perhaps he put more emphasis or pressure on his play just because it was the final round. He may have thought about the implications of winning before he actually won. Whatever the answers may be, this guy must realize how to deal with his thought process and help ease his uncomfortable circumstances so he can eliminate anything interfering with good play. That is why I am such a fan of routine and structure.

As we have said before, our unconscious is primal. When we are put into a situation that makes us extremely anxious, our conscious mind has to help. When we are afraid and nervous, we only recognize the problems; we do not always understand them. Positive reinforcement from our cognitive process can help ease the pain. This reinforcement can come from self-talk, routine, mechanical structure or other people. Do you remember being sick when you were young? You felt terrible until your mother began caring for you. Just having her there made everything better. The golf course can be a lonely place. Tour players have it made if they have a good caddy in their employment. Caddies usually are the best psychologists and teachers of the game. They can be worth every penny unless they just carry the bag.

There are many people who are not very tough or self-reliant and need the stability of another person to help them get through the rough patches. Existentially, this is why everyone needs someone in their life. Companionship is very important. Other people complement our shortcomings if we allow them. A good caddy, teacher, family or friends can add a wonderful support system to our lives. These folks that lack that mental toughness usually have a great deal of negativity toward themselves.

Negative self-talk interrupts positive execution. So does our self-talk need to be negative? Self-talk should be constructive rather than destructive. If we do not build ourselves strong, we will remain weak. Conversations that happen in our own mind need to be clear and meaningful, not filled with irrational or unrealistic thoughts. They need to be focused on what is important to us personally and what we already know. We have an innate ability to reinforce positive behavior just by giving ourselves the opportunity to grow psychologically. Our limits need to be known, but we also stop way before we need to at times. Our mind says one thing, our bodies say another. Make sure that mind and body agree on the purpose. You can talk yourself into just about anything if you are listening. Do not tune yourself out. Listening to positive and constructive advice coming from within our own psyche can help our process become very clear. Clarity is bliss. How do we achieve ultimate clarity? A sound and practiced routine is essential.

Our unconscious is very needy. It reminds us how vulnerable we actually are. A well-organized pre-shot routine will help diminish the unwanted feelings that occur when we feel threatened. Since repetition is the key to learning, learning is the process necessary to allow cognition to work.

Simply put, find a routine before you play your shot. It could include cap tips, pant pulls, shirt grabs, left foot right foot or so on. The key is to do the same thing over and over again. The pre-shot routine tells the unconscious that everything is going to be alright. Routine allows us to think without thinking and feel without trying to feel.

Finally, our swing structure plays an enormous role in fighting the neuroses established in the unconscious. Our cognition can override our nervousness by telling us what to do. Remember the unconscious needs to be comforted. If we feel anxiety in an uncomfortable setting, we have to have something to combat that nervousness. I have used my knowledge of swing mechanics to overcome any type of doubt on the golf course. Having swing structure you can repeat and use as a key can help anyone overcome unwanted psychological distress that occurs before, during or after a round of golf.

This is the case for any sport that requires idleness before play. Think of the free throw shooter. He steps to line with the game in the balance, goes through his routine and shoots the ball the same way every time. Think of the field goal kicker, baseball pitcher, archer, tennis player (during the serve) or swimmer. In order to deal with unconscious pressure, we must have mechanisms in place to deal with neurotic behavior. Recognize that we all have anxiety, and understand that is a good thing. It is how we react to tough times that prove us better or worse than the other guy.

If our conscious moments are filled with clarity that usually indicates that our unconscious self is under control. Do not ever ignore your emotions. Seize the opportunity to understand them and make yourself stronger through positive cognitive self-talk. After all, being good at something starts with being good to the self.

Lessons Learned:

- Our unconscious is simple minded. It knows the activity at hand like hitting the ball, and we are not aware that it already knows what to do. Our conscious mind can complicate everything if we are not clear about our objectives.
- Anxiety is not created in the unconscious, it is just housed there. Anxious moments are usually remembered by the unconscious through activities that cause us distress.
- Self-talk does not have to be negative. Our cognitive thoughts need to reflect healthy conversations that build our confidence and our ability to deal with anxious moments. We need to recognize our "bad" feelings and deal with them. This is the most important part of overcoming destructive behavior. We may not ever be aware of the unconscious traps we set for ourselves so we must recognize what worries us.
- A repetitive swing motion is a key to letting the unconscious relax during anxious moments. A sound swing structure allows the individual to overcome the parts of the round of golf that create discomfort. A good swing is a default for poor judgment. Sound swing mechanics sometimes do not need to be recognized by the conscious mind, but swing structure is very important.
- The ultimate in great golf play would be for the individual player to hit shot after shot and never really be aware of what needs to be practiced. The only negative is if the player has no idea how to recoup lost performance and does not know where he/she needs to start in order to regain form.

In my mind's eye, this is what God intended when golf courses were developed.

II. Peace of Mind

"Knowing yourself is the beginning of all wisdom."
-Aristotle

Trust is an essential emotional, spiritual and psychological key that is necessary for a person to find inner peace. That inner peace, or awareness, will allow us to act with an understanding that trust can be stronger than our doubts. Trust is a learned behavior, whether it pertains to relationships, individual growth or activities. When trying to achieve trust, it is helpful to practice a process that allows us to achieve this type of awareness.

Learning can be an ingredient of this practice, especially as it relates to golf. Though there are many variables to learning, it is not complicated. The learning that takes place in each individual helps to build a foundation for growth. Remember that knowledge can be very powerful, and it is what we do with the knowledge that is important. If we are receptive and still, a powerful form of learning can be very helpful in achieving trust.

The first thing that any golfer needs to understand is that the ball will always travel where the club face is aimed at the moment of impact as it relates to the geometry of the swing plane. If you have a problem controlling ball flight, you must learn what causes ball flight and correct it. How many times have you played a round of golf, felt wonderful on the practice tee and then once you reached the course lost shot after shot to poor ball striking?

As an instructor, I cannot tell you how many times I have heard this. The ball must be directed by the club face, in line with the desired plane line at the moment of impact. A negative mental process can cause poor ball striking, but it is usually poor mechanics. In addition, poor mechanics can result in poor putting and chipping, creating a high score.

Bad mechanics also create the worst mental condition of all: insecurity and a lack of trust. If players do not understand their mechanics, they will have limited peace of mind on the course. By having a mechanically sound stroke pattern, also including short shots, you can begin to trust your swing.

Trust is essential. It is the primary condition for attaining emotional security. Trust allows uninhibited performance. All great players try to produce a trusting swing. It gives them the peace of mind necessary to play every day and compete under pressure. Trust is what drives most decisions we make in our life. It is a very powerful state of being. Have you ever been totally trusting of something in your life? To feel that we can count on something or someone gives us a great deal of comfort.

Trust is also a very powerful form of learning. Abraham Maslow, one of the foremost thinkers in humanistic psychology, said that in order to achieve personal growth necessary for what he called "self-actualization," a person had to experience a dynamic form of learning. Whether we are playing golf, investing money or seeing a doctor, trust plays a vital role in giving us the peace of mind to do anything. If we learn to trust ourselves and our process, we can learn to trust our golf game and experience true development. .

How do we achieve trust in our golf game? One way is to establish a process that repeats itself and provides the desired feedback. The process must provide information to the learner that is understandable as well. If we repeat and understand the process at the same time, we grow comfortable even if the outcomes are not always positive. Obviously, if our outcomes are always negative, our trust factor goes away and insecurity becomes more probable.

Understanding the process intellectually leads to a mechanical feel. So I search for the knowledge that allows me to understand. The laws of ball flight are explainable. Certain mechanics fit certain ball flights. A number of swings work very well even when they are different. Though many instructors try to teach the same process, there is rarely a standard procedure for every player. Cures for faulty ball flight have to fit the ailment. Our body knows if we are out of balance through our nervous system, so there is always manipulation of the swing if it is not mechanically sound.

The mind is complex, but it recognizes that hitting the ball is the primary objective. If you have a faulty mechanical procedure, your brain will process the problem and tell you through physical discomfort and emotional insecurity that something needs to be fixed. This causes emotional fear if you do not know how to fix the problem, and that is why structure is important. A sound physical structure will lead to your ability to repeat a swing with certainty. This leads to repetition of ball flight and the belief that you can do it again. When a player has the proper knowledge base, accompanied by a process that is executed positively over and over again, it creates the equation for confidence. Knowledge plus execution equals confidence.

My experiences on the golf course used to be filled with emotional strain and distrust, which led to a lack of desired results. I had limited trust in my golf swing, my ability as a player and possibly even as a person. I can remember being in tournament situations panic-stricken over particular shots. I played scared. There were many shots that I knew I could not hit because I did not trust my swing. I was competing in a tournament in Florida one spring and I was playing well. I came to my 12th hole and found my second shot about 200 yards from the green. I felt like I needed to hit a three-iron to reach the green, but I was very uncomfortable hitting this club because I did not hit long irons very well. So instead of hitting another club I hit the three-iron, to prove to myself I could hit it. The shot went into a bunker on the right side of the green. I was so angry after the shot, I allowed that one swing to ruin the rest of my round.

I had incorporated a deeply paranoid state of mind that did not allow me to play to my capabilities. I used to have instructors tell me, "Just trust your swing." I would say to myself, "Are you kidding? The ball is going everywhere." Once I had an instructor tell me, "SEE IT, FEEL IT, and TRUST IT." I saw it, it looked terrible and I was surely NOT going to trust it. So how did I develop trust and confidence in my game, with this state of paranoid awareness? It is easier for some than others, but for me, developing trust became a process.

Every accomplished player in the game of golf has to learn to develop trust. Understanding your fears and learning to trust yourself and your swing will allow you to manage your emotions. Learning to trust can create a divine awareness. For me, trust came from understanding my mechanics and knowing my ball flight tendencies.

Some will argue that thinking mechanics undermine any positive outcome of your shots. That is nonsense. Let's be realistic: Everyone has swing thoughts. Whether it is a nursery rhyme or deeply complicated mechanical thoughts, everyone thinks of something. Players make excessive thinking an excuse because the things they are thinking about do not work. Those professional golfers who deny thought are now folding sweaters at a nearby pro shop.

There can be times when players focus so much on parts of their swing that they forget to play. I agree that this can be a problem; however, I would much rather see a player focused on a learned process than just freewheeling and wishing for their ball to go where they want. I remember running into a professional player who did not want to know anything about his swing. I thought to myself, "He won't play professionally very long." He didn't. By not wanting to know about his process, he could hide his insecurity. He felt like his greatest fear, which was losing his playing privileges, would disappear if he did nothing to learn about his own game. Obviously, he was mistaken.

A thought process has to be executed in order for someone to have a trusting swing or trust in him or herself. In golf, that process is usually physical. I do not advocate cluttering the mind with unnecessary mechanical thought. In fact, we should try to eliminate worrisome thoughts and not do the first thing that comes to our mind.

I am reminded of a collegiate player that was struggling with his game who sought the help of a sport psychologist. The advice given was to the do the first thing that came into your mind to eliminate indecision. So this young man went onto the course and did the first thing that came to his mind. Ironically, the first thing that came to his mind was not always productive. Needless to say, this young man struggled with his game.

Building trust is a matter of dependence on the outcome. In sports, we cannot always control the outcome of a situation, but golf is one of the few sports where we have some control. Do not give that control away by being irrational. Building trust is a process of building a repeating swing that you understand mechanically and intellectually. In order for me to build a repeating swing, I watched hours of video of my own technique. I had no fear of seeing my swing because I knew it needed improvement. I was strong and very athletic, but hit the ball short and off-line. After seeing my swing on video, I began to incorporate basics of the swing based on facts and law. This was a huge step. The ball can actually go where you want it to go if you swing correctly according to a swing model. Facts are an amazing contributor to an efficient process.

Establishing a swing model is important. Many different swings work, but sometimes we do not know what makes them work. I would advise you to establish a swing model that has minimal moving parts. Fewer movements mean less chance for error. Limited head movement and limited weight shifting is preferable for all players, from the professional to the amateur. Establish where you want to aim the ball. Choose a particular ball flight and then begin to work on your swing model. An example of a particular ball flight would be a "draw" or a right to left ball flight. This swing would use this ball flight as the guide to hitting the player's most repetitive shot.

Why is this important? If a player has a shot of choice, he or she can know where the ball is traveling. Even if the player misses, he or she has hit that particular shot enough to understand they can trust in themselves and the swing. There is great comfort in knowing where the missed shot is going. Many players have made a wonderful living by knowing their own misses.

Any ball flight will work if the swing model is repeated. Whatever the ball flight, learn it and understand it. Then you can repeat that stroke pattern over and over again. The key ingredient is establishing a framework of repeatable processes that can get you hitting the ball at the target with consistency. If you hit the ball pretty straight and are trying to learn to hit the ball further, learn what causes distance and apply the necessary physical techniques in order to accomplish more distance.

The only reason people are afraid to think and learn is because they do not trust the information. In many cases, instructors do not provide adequate answers. Many golf instructors are not good players themselves and have limited training. The reason most instructors discourage thinking is because they simply do not know how to help. Golf becomes trial and error. This is a very dangerous approach to learning. Imagine if we had the same approach to medicine and did not try to research the causes for illness. This is a dramatic, but true comparison.

Furthermore, understand that building peace of mind is relevant to knowledge. Knowledge about golf exists. Learning about your swing and creating a process that works can help to eliminate the psychological and emotional issues that keep us from succeeding on the course. Knowledge is indeed power. Understanding this simple truth will prove to be a valuable ally when trying to improve your golf game. Peace of mind is an awareness that provides us a healthy perspective about fulfillment in our lives. It is a condition that we find in people that are truly happy.

Lessons Learned:

- In order to trust and achieve peace of mind, we must overcome the idea that thinking is a bad thing which should be avoided. Knowledge is power and execution is the reinforcement that leads to confidence.
- Do your best, whether you are tour professional or amateur, to find a qualified instructor that understands ball flight. If he or she does not use video, do not study with them. That is like going to a doctor who does not believe in an x-ray.
- The key to learning is repetition.
- The key to trust is seeing the desired results. Once you see the results, you will feel good about the process.
- Choose the mechanical process and learn. It will transform your game. Peace of mind will follow.
- Remember to use simple techniques; do not try to simplify something complex without a cause and effect explanation.

Ben Hogan had the best golf stroke of all time.

III. Overcoming the Ego

"Many could forgo heavy meals, a full wardrobe, a fine house, etc. It is the ego they cannot forgo."
-Mohandas Gandhi

Having an educational background in Psychological Counseling has given me exposure to a great deal of research. The Diagnostics and Statistical Manuel (DSM) outlines psychological illness. It is a challenging read, but also very interesting. Most of the psychiatric conditions listed in the DSM are contingent upon pre-disposition for neurological and chemical illness, genetic factors and environment. However, one of the main causes of psychological distress is our ego that resides in our conscious thought. In other words, that little person inside us all, or our ego, creates expectations that try to control our actions, which in effect try to control our outcomes.

If we really think about it, we create most of our own distress by just suggesting to ourselves the way things ought to be. That is called a value system, which is created by our ego. For instance, a golfer may say, "I should hit my driver 300 yards." Now, if you are a professional player maybe, but if you're not, you must think a lot more of your ability than you probably should.

Great expectations are wonderful if you have prepared for the desired objective. I had a student who came to me complaining about lack of distance. I started by asking him how far he hit his seven-iron. He confidently told me between 145 and 150 yards. This gentleman was slightly built, weighing maybe 150 pounds and was in his 60s. I took 30 or so balls and said to him, "Let's see how many balls you hit 145 yards with your seven-iron." After he hit a few shots, I could see the issues.

We walked out to the range and located the balls. He had hit one ball 135 yards and the rest were between 120 and 130 yards. I asked him why he thought he hit his seven-iron 145 to 150 yards. It was the ego inside of him creating his expectations. This poor fellow played the course thinking from 150 yards he needed to play a seven-iron. He was about two clubs short. After I put a five-iron in his hand, he hit more greens from 150 yards because he was hitting a club that he was capable of physically, releasing all the faulty expectations of his ego. There were things mechanically he could do to hit the ball further. However, it would take several days of practice, so I just politely told him to hit his five-iron from 150 yards and we would work on his ball hitting and gain more distance over time. His expectations for ball hitting were unrealistic at this point and time. If he were to expect to hit his seven-iron 130 yards, what would be wrong with that? Nobody ever checks the distance you hit each club on the scorecard at the end of the round.

After hours and hours of practice, you probably have quite high expectations for your game. Our ego creates an ideal golf game that sometimes is hard to achieve. I will always remember the misguided expectations that have plagued my golfing life. No matter how well I played, I found failure in my score. I was setting myself up for disappointment every time. Satisfaction was never attained.

After realizing I could live with myself on the golf course, I suddenly thought, "Maybe I am not going to hit every shot perfect." A huge burden had been lifted from my shoulders. I had just become aware that my ego was creating these unrealistic expectations. I am going to miss a shot every now and then, and there is nothing wrong with that. Sometimes our golf games and our lives do not produce perfection. By being aware of this, our unrealistic expectations can be diminished, and our ego can work to our benefit.

Understanding that our expectations will determine how we approach the game of golf and the game of life is very important. Expectations will decide our practice, our play, our instruction and the way we manage ourselves around the golf course. We need to create expectations that work to our benefit, not allow our ego to suggest unattainable expectations. How do manage our expectations? First, determine what you want from the game through a statement of intentions. Golf can be nothing more than an emotional and physical exercise for some people, a social activity for others or even a way to provide a living.

In my golfing life, I put so much effort into the game that I became distressed if I did not perform up to my standards. My ego was producing expectations that were very difficult to achieve. When I analyze my golf history, I begin to realize my errors. I had no practice routine, limited tournament experience and a golf swing that needed some fine-tuning. Golf was so important to me that it became work instead of a game that I loved to play for fun. It was supposed to be enjoyable, pleasing and filled with joy, but that was not what it was becoming.

We must learn to enjoy the game and approach it with a joyful enthusiasm. What other sport can be played and shared by all skill levels and all ages? It is competitive under the correct format for all players. Golf should be approached as something we want to do, not something we have to do. Learn to accept what the game gives you. It is a very difficult game that requires days and years of practice and patience. Golf is not a game that can be picked up immediately. We must see the game as a challenge, rather than something we have to do in order to fulfill our ego.

Expectations are not limited to the game itself. We must also realize our individual ability levels. Understanding ability is not settling for mediocrity. It is winning before you get started. My favorite baseball player as a youngster was Pete Rose. Pete was a guy who did not hit for power even though he could, had limited arm strength and could not run with a great deal of speed. Pete Rose understood what he could do best and became one of the greatest baseball players of all time. If I ever had to start a team, it would be with Pete.

Understanding ability level will help you approach the game from a rational point of view. Many of us are never going to hit the ball 300 yards in the air. There are only a few players in world that can do that. I'm really not sure that if I could hit the ball that far it would be a great benefit to my game anyway. It is this kind of rational thought that helps manage our expectations on and off the golf course.

I am not advocating reducing expectations to the point of settling for mediocrity. I am saying realize your individual strengths as a player.

Analyze the amount of time you can give the game, and see how much time you spend practicing. This will help you enjoy the game more and play better. If you understand your expectations and understand what you are trying to accomplish, I can almost assure you your scores will be better and you will enjoy the game.

Another ingredient that helps us deal with expectations is expecting to play well. Never go to the golf course with the idea that you are not going to play well today. If you expect to play well and are optimistic about the outcome, you can overcome many of the weaknesses in your game. Every time the tee goes in the ground, tip your cap to the crowd and feel as though you're there to win. It seems contradictory to say keep your ego in check and then expect to play well. Part of achieving your expectations is expecting to succeed, but understand how you are going to do it and don't set yourself up to fail.

I am reminded of a professional player who recently has had a great deal of success. He nearly lost his card a few years ago, but he made some swing changes and finally recaptured excellent form. After having an outstanding game, he felt like he should rise to one of the top 10 players in the world. His kind of thinking is a little dangerous. His expectations needed to be kept in check or each time he did not get a top 10 finish, he had failed. There is nothing wrong with expecting to play well. But there is a difference in expecting to play well and poor judgment. Expect to continue to improve and do the things necessary to do so. If you are the 150th ranked player in the world and want to go to 10th after one good year, be assured that may be a shock to your system.

Expectations are either a great help or a great detriment. The personal ego can affect our expectations, but other people can also be a big influence as well. We try to compensate for our shortcomings through expectations. We constantly try to make ourselves feel better by exaggerating our abilities just to satisfy our ego. This is where we allow our self-image to affect our performance. Self-image is completely different form self-esteem. Self-image is based on how we think others view us in our environment. And this perception is very powerful.

If we think about it, this has a lot to do with how we approach the game of golf. For instance, it never ceases to amaze me how people will distort their handicap. It can go in either direction. In most cases, those people who believe their handicap is lower than it actually is cause most problems. They never play to their full potential due to the fact that they always have a distorted reality.

I had a student who would always come to the range and coach me. He was always telling me how he could interpret my instruction based on some sort of feel. That can be a valid way of interpreting instruction, but this was not the case here. It took all my patience to remain still and teach this man. I just wanted him to admit that he was about a 15 handicap. He was convinced he was much better, which made for limited progress. He tried to hit the ball as hard as he could, which made his technique erratic. The more I taught him, the more I understood that he suffered from self-image issues. Here was a very capable person who thought of himself and his golf game very irrationally.

My strategy was very simple. I played a number of rounds with him after each lesson to show how his method did not work and how mine would. I tried to convince him that distance was necessary, but not for him. We played the golf course with his irons only and from as far back as we could play on the tee markers. This strategy did two things: It deflated his ego and made him concentrate on the game. We had reasonable success. But what I had found was that he was more impressionable by other golfers than concentrating on his game. For instance, when he did hit a good tee shot, he would hear things like, "That was a big one" or "You killed that one!" He got a tremendous amount of satisfaction from other people's suggestions, which guided his expectations.

Golf is an individual game based on score. There are many times that individual effort is overcome by faulty expectations completely based on a concept that does not exist. Other people play a significant role in how we perceive the game of golf as well as other life events.

This is good advice for adult golfers as well. Those players who expect to play well according to their individual strengths which they recognize are indeed the most successful. We have to make sure the ego is a productive part of our games by realizing what we are capable of when we play. Faulty expectation can be very destructive. Instead, we must learn to play with favorable expectations that complement our talent.

Lessons Learned:

- Expectations play a vital role in the outcome of our golf. We must now consider a plan and how we can apply appropriate expectations to our golf game.
- First, have a private statement of intentions. Intentions will guide how you expect to play. Then realize your mechanical or physical abilities and your experience.
- Expect to play well, but always provide yourself with a perception that will allow you to adjust frustrating outcomes.
- One unfortunate round of golf does not define your play. Think of how many holes you will continue to play in your life and try to keep that into perspective. Think about the things that you do well and play to those strengths.
- Develop a strong self-image by using concepts that are based on your thoughts and feelings about yourself and do not allow other people to help develop your golf image. Your golf game should be based on the rules and procedures of the game not the development of a faulty perception that your peers influence.
- Golf is only a game. It does not define you, but it can tell many things about your character and how you approach other life events.

Clay Hamrick and the search for a golf guru

Don McNay

MCNAY'S MUSINGS

Abraham Shakespeare did not have much luck in finding a financial advisor.

The dead body of the Florida lottery winner was found in 2009 in the backyard of Dee Dee Moore's boyfriend. Under a slab of concrete.

Moore, who served as Shakespeare's advisor, is on trial this month for his murder.

Shakespeare did not do an extensive search to find his advisor. After winning a $17 million lottery jackpot, Moore connected with Shakespeare after asking a policeman to trace Shakespeare's license plate.

I'm writing a new book called, "Life Lessons from the Lottery." Lottery winners have the same problems average people do, but their problems are magnified by the large amounts of money they receive.

People who get lousy financial advice normally don't wind up dead. But they often wind up broke.

I have a simple rule for finding a financial advisor. Don't be that person's most important client.

If you get a $100 million windfall, find an advisor who has worked with $150 million.

It gets complicated finding an advisor outside the financial field.

You can't easily quantify whether a person is a good teacher, plumber or ballet instructor.

I spent most of the Christmas season in the hospital. I made a list of things to do when I got better and playing golf was one of them.

Self-taught as a teenager, I went through long periods when I didn't play golf at all and eight years ago, decided to give the game up completely.

Coming back at age 53, I was not golfing until I could play without embarrassing myself.

That is where Clay Hamrick came into my life.

I've been working with Anne Parton, who runs a personal-assistant business called IAssist, with entrepreneurs as her primary client base. Anne has been a personal assistant to several high-powered people, and I had hired her to help me coordinate my last book tour.

I kept her on to organize the rest of my life.

Anne sat down with me, developed a comprehensive list of what I wanted to do as a golfer and how much time I needed to schedule.

Then, she went out to interview golf professionals. She came back with Clay Hamrick.

I would have never found Clay on my own. He is the head pro at Battlefield Golf Course, a small public course. Not the place where I'd expect to find the ultimate golf guru.

It turns out that Clay has an incredible background, including being the head pro at a top-100 course. He graduated from Eastern Kentucky University, married a woman from a prominent local family, and they moved back to the region to raise their children.

A lucky break for me.

On the surface, Clay and I could not be more opposite. He is incredibly intense, handsome, in perfect physical condition and impeccably dressed. I'm none of the above.

As it turns out, we have a lot in common. He is incredibly well read, a deep thinker and an absolute student of the game. He pushes a concept called the "Stack and Tilt" system, which is perfect for a middle-aged man getting back in the game.

Under Clay's high-strung exterior is a deeply caring man with the heart of a lion.

Turn to **GOLF**, *page C2*

GOLF

Continued from page A1

He is a passionate advocate for how golf can improve my overall well-being and physical health. He gets truly excited when I make progress and posts films of the results on my Facebook page.

He uses every type of modern technology to analyze and improve my game.

He also had a revelation that changed my golf swing. Clay's uncle, Dave Tomlin, was a star relief pitcher for the Cincinnati Reds during the "Big Red Machine" era of my youth. He looked at me and said, "Imagine my uncle is pitching to you and hit the ball to Dave Concepcion."

Once I developed that visual picture, I started whacking the ball.

I played my first nine holes at the West Baden resort in French Lick, Indiana. Not an easy course, but I knocked in two birdies.

The last time I had two birdies in a round, Bill Clinton was president.

I was so excited, I called Clay from the middle of the golf course.

He, Anne and I have an extensive plan for improving my game over the next two years. It also relates to how I am starting to lose weight and do something that does not involve an easy chair.

Clay has made a big impact on my life and become a good friend.

The key was figuring out what I wanted and finding a top notch person to implement the plan.

If Abraham Shakespeare had done the same, he might be alive, enjoying his lottery winnings, instead of dying an early death.

IV. Spiritual Accomplishment

"But the Fruit of the Spirit is love, joy, peace, patience, kindness, goodness, faith, gentleness and self-control. Against such things there is no law."
-The Apostle Paul

The 20th century psychologist Albert Ellis invented a process for psychological therapy called RET, or Rational Emotive Therapy. Ellis contends that most of the psychological traps that people suffer from are created from what he called "crooked thinking." Ellis was a very dynamic therapist who could be offensive during a therapy session. He would challenge the way people construct their own thoughts.

If Ellis were a sports psychologist, he would have a field day with golfers. In my experience as an instructor and player, I have never come across a more crooked thinking group of athletes than those who play golf. Many people lose all clear perspective on the golf course. How many times have you played a round of golf, played your shot and then just couldn't believe what you had done? It happens all time. Irrational types of thought patterns all come from innate insecurities that we all have about ourselves.

When golfers start to think crookedly, they exhibit specific characteristics. They become physically nervous, display anxiety, their breathing becomes rapid and short and, more importantly, they are consumed by indecisiveness. The indecisiveness is the most telling because it shows how we really think and feel about our own abilities. When we start to think crookedly and our results are not as expected, we are consumed with anger. That anger is what tells us how disappointed we are with ourselves.

Crooked thinking comes from many places. Being unprepared creates crooked thinking. Golf, as with many other endeavors, takes a great deal of preparation. Constant ball hitting, putting and short shot practice are just some aspects of golf that need to be practiced. Other not so obvious things that need practiced are patience, good nature and self-control. Many things that you read about golf psychology all deal with how to stay in the present and how to go through a pre-shot routine. But most of us need to go a little deeper to really understand presence. Being totally committed to staying in the present allows us to eliminate some of the irrational thoughts that consume our thinking. Patience is one the tools that can help define how we stay in the moment.

Patience is a virtue. It has also been identified as a "fruit of the spirit" as mentioned in the Bible in the Book of Galatians. Patience is the single most important trait of anyone who has ever done anything well. A lack of patience has to be one of the biggest threats to efficient golf. Most of the best players in golf, present and past, display the greatest amount of patience and always talk about how important the patient mind is to their success. Patience allows us to create strategy and also helps us to cope with disappointment.

The best way to be patient is to be aware of the now and disregard our future. Patience comes in many forms. We do not have to be calm to be patient. Patience can involve passion and intensity. On the golf course, we should try not to put future outcomes on our game. I see players all the time try to create scoring instead of playing the game that is given to them. This is the epitome of the impatient approach that leads to golfing destruction.

The best example of the patient golfer is the player that wins the US Open. Not only is the US Open usually set up very challenging, the self-induced pressure that players place on a national championship is an absolute example of crooked thinking. No tournament should have more importance than the other. Great players are defined by winning majors, but at the same time certain championships should not be the entire focus if a player wants to have longevity playing the game.

I once heard a sports writer say that one of the current players should not be considered one of the greatest of all time because he did not have an exceptional major championship record. That of course is nonsense. All players that play professionally are great players. If you get paid to play golf, you are a great player. Certain tournaments like the US Open require the greatest amount of patience. The course is difficult because that satisfies the amateur's ego, and the self-induced pressure of a national title brings about a certain kind of self-talk. In order to win the golf tournament, you have to plod along hitting your ball on the fairways and on the greens and minimize your mistakes. That takes a tremendous amount of psychological stamina.

Some players usually win the US Open because someone else lost. The full testimony of patience is to do your best and see what happens. Sometimes you never know. For the amateur playing the Sunday Nassau, it is the same process.

Other than my father and my son, there is one gentleman who I love to play golf with more than any other person. I would play with this guy everyday just because he is the ultimate competitor. He fluctuates between an 8 and 13 handicap. This man is the essence of eternal optimism on the golf course. He takes every chance he can manage and takes no chances he cannot. He truly understands the game and knows he is as good as he is going to get. He has the best golf mind of any amateur I have ever seen, and he has never taken a lesson.

I remember playing a match against him and his partner in Ireland. (The golf courses in Ireland are notoriously difficult.) All the way around the course, I was winning the game. I had to give him a bunch of strokes, but I was still in control of the match. Somehow we got down to the last hole with the wagering riding on a particular press that would swing all the money his way. Both of our partners were in their pockets, so it was just us. I had hit the ball right down the middle of the fairway. He had hit his tee shot well left and had a very difficult approach to the green. He knew he had to make the shot of a lifetime to hit the ball next to the pin. He played safe to the back of the green. I thought, "This guy is playing for the tie. Unbelievable, he never does that!"

I stood over my second shot, fully knowing I had the win in the bag and hit the shot about fifteen or so feet to the right of the pin. I walked to the green chastising my opponent for playing the safe shot. I cannot remember exactly what I said, but it was something along the line of him being chicken excrement. He said nothing. When we got to the green, he was a least 60 feet away, over swales and turns. If he two-putted, it was going to be a great par. He kept looking at the putt over and over and talking to his caddie. I rudely interrupted with my usual candor: "Today, please."

He hit the putt, and as I watched his ball come down the hill, over the swale, around the turn and fall right into the hole, I just about fell over. I could not believe it. He made an impossible play on an impossible hole at an impossible time. I had to give him a shot on that hole, my putt was meaningless. So I did what any reasonable man would do: I swore at him, threw my ball into the ocean and got my wallet out. He did nothing except say thank you after I paid him.

At no time did my opponent try to press the issue. He played patiently and good things happened. That is almost perfect golf. He played what the game gave him and did not let any crooked thoughts enter into his mind. He was filled with complete presence. He did not try to make an impossible shot or ever doubt that he could not stay in the game. Lots of good things happen when you play golf the patient way.

Patience can be a learned behavior. The wise man learns from the mistakes of his past, and the fool does the same destructive things over and over trying to achieve different results. This, according to Einstein, is the definition of insanity. Avoid that if you can. We learn from our environment and from our experiences. The Psalmist says that the wisest of men learns from his mistakes, but the wisest of all men learns from the mistakes of others. Patience is the culmination of experience and a learned spirit.

Another key ingredient to eliminating crooked thinking is to improve your nature on the golf course. Our nature is defined by how we act or behave. I am not suggesting that we have an "aw shucks" attitude or laugh and skip around, but we should try to play with an inner joy.

If we are distracted, angry, depressed or any of the distractions that plague us on a daily basis, it is likely your golf will suffer. Golf is difficult. We need to enjoy our golf for our mental and physical health if nothing else.

Improving our nature is very simple. We have to make a decision on what we want from our golf game. Understand that a negative nature does not help. It only weakens us. We have to take the joyous approach that eliminates senseless acts of anger or frustration. Our nature on the golf course does not define us. But it creates a perception of the self and has a great deal to do with how other people view us.

I had a good friend in college who was an avid club thrower and complainer. I learned a handful of good club throwing techniques from my friend. I did not mind the club throwing; I minded him not realizing his ability. My friend started complaining from the time he teed off to the time he signed his card. Obviously he had a great deal of trouble getting a friendly game. I loved him personally, but hated playing golf with him. I took it upon myself one day to explain to him that his complaining and club throwing did nothing but hurt his game, but it also was driving his teammates away. He had no idea that he was offending anyone and no idea how miserable he actually was. After he improved his nature by allowing a little joy to penetrate his soul, his game became much better and his teammates were excited to play with him.

As we stated earlier, golf has way too many variables. We have the opportunity to control many of those variables through practice and knowledge. A poor attitude only adds to the variables that cause bad golf. My martial arts instructor used to tell me constantly you cannot fight angry for very long. You might be able to fight mad for a little while, but it just takes too much energy to be angry and still compete. It is real easy to get hurt if you're "fighting mad." This holds true for the golf course as well.

The best golf I ever played, I played by really not caring about the outcome. There was no future. I tried to hit the fairways, hit the greens and not make any big scores. The only time I cared what I scored was on the last hole when I figured out I could win. I suddenly decided to think crookedly and hit my tee shot out of bounds. I doubled the last hole and thought for sure I lost the tournament. Lots of good things happen when you play golf the right way. I won by two shots. I don't know what made me change for that day, but it sure made golf more fun. I had no anxiety, less fear and I looked forward to playing each and every shot. I realized my nature was keeping me from playing the kind of golf I wanted to play. I was unhappy every time I played.

Seems strange, doesn't it? This is not uncommon for many people. Many people are chronic malcontents. They are unhappy just because they are used to it. They feel as though they were meant to be unhappy. This is the epitome of crooked thinking. Change your nature when you come to the course if you feel like golf is a struggle. Do your best to enjoy the game even if it is your job. Even on your worst day, the golf course is a good place to be and an even better place to spend time with your family or friends. It is an existential paradise. Golf is a game that is designed to promote happiness, fairness and health. Just being outside does you good, not to mention some friendly competition or a walk with your kids. Golf is good for everyone, so every time you tee it up, enjoy it.

Learning to control one's self is a major undertaking. As the Book of Galatians says, self-control is a "fruit of the spirit." I firmly believe that someone who has control of his or her emotions will have an abundance of success. Relationships will be easier, occupations will be much less stressful and we will feel happier most of the time. Again, a lack of self-control tells a great deal about a person's ability to cope with life's events. One of the reasons self-control on the golf course is so difficult is because there are so many components to the game and we are always fighting the ego. We can hit a good tee shot and then shank a ball out of bounds or hit a ball a foot from the hole and miss the putt. The game overwhelms people because they cannot control all of those variables. Having self-control will allow you to approach the game with clarity and give you the strength to give up control.

For instance, amateurs have limited control over their process when playing the game due to their physical ability. They play shots off the tee with clubs they should never consider, and then play approach shots to green locations that should be played to the center of greens instead of at the pins. It is much easier to play to your strengths, but most of us just can't. Many have no self-control because they have this crooked/irrational concept of themselves, which is the ego, rolling through their minds about hitting the par five in two, driving a green, knocking it tight, holing it out or some other grandiose futuristic thought that has not happened.

Self-control is not just controlling your anger. Self-control is about controlling your emotional and psychological process. Sometimes anger helps. It can make you more determined, but much of the time it is very destructive. I do not condone folks throwing a temper fit on the golf course, even though I have thrown my fair share. I especially want all junior golfers to know that getting angry is normal; just do not let anger be destructive to yourself, others or your game. Getting angry can exercise many demons. If you eat bad food, it is better to throw up and get rid of the sickness before it gets in your system.

I never discourage folks from feeling angry. Anger is an emotion that tells a story and needs to be recognized. The problem with anger is how you use it. If you are destructive, that's not productive. If you internalize anger and dismiss it, that is no good either. (Many psychotics are very angry people on the inside, but not visibly angry on the outside.) Anger creates more crooked thinking than any other emotion except for fear. This is because fear is usually linked to anger. Learning to defeat the destructive nature of anger is the essence of self-control. Anger needs to be focused into positive productive energy.

The angriest person I have ever seen on the golf course is the game's best player. He plays with an inferno of fire that bubbles through his being like a bomb that can go off at any time. When he is disgusted or angry, he gets it out and then moves on with a more focus and determined attitude than ever before. Ben Hogan seemed to be much the same way. He was not externally angry, but he was internally very determined. He was curt, quiet and, from what I have read, very unapproachable on the golf course. I did not know Hogan, so I cannot say for sure, but my perception is that he was very determined, had his own way about him and really did not care much for what anyone else thought.

Those people who can control themselves are the folks that can persevere on the golf course. It is fine to display emotion, but we need to use our emotions to our benefit. Self-control is an element of the soul that will be of great benefit to us in many ways.

Practicing self-control, patience and playing with joy is a major challenge for many of us. If we lack these spirit-building qualities, our nature will always be restless. There is so much time to think during a round of golf and no reaction time, because the ball does not move. Doing things that make the essence of our spirit or nature stronger is very important.

Many times during a round of golf, we find ourselves projecting our score way too far in advance. This is not a good practice. We think to ourselves, "If I can birdie this one, par the next one and maybe hit the par five in two, WOW! I may shoot my best score ever." Those who live in the past forget about their future and regret their now. Those who live life regretting will be truly unhappy, and the accomplishments they attained will never be enough to help them overcome their individual regrets. When playing a game of golf, never think about what could have been or what could be or what happened three holes ago. There is only now. You are going to play several games in your life, so it just does not matter. You never want to risk your now for the past or the future. Never look back except to learn, and never look forward except to dream.

Be patient with yourself and understand that nothing is accomplished all at once. Golf is to be played one shot at a time and one hole at a time. Trying to predict the future puts the present at risk. Irrationality usually is present when you are focused on everything except what is happening now. Irrationality creates a feeling that causes a negative comfort that carries over into all parts of our being.

It always amazes me when a player makes consecutive birdies. The best players have no idea when they have made five or six birdies in a row. When I was playing, if I made two or three birdies in a row, I would think the apocalypse was just around the corner. This is an example of being out of my comfort zone because I had not scored multiple birdies in a row very often and that triggered too much thinking. I would think my good score would go away, and it usually did.

The game of golf is a taker. It will take your confidence, your dignity, your self-control and your patience. By employing the fruits of the spirit, you can take everything the game gives you because you are peaceful and comfortable with the outcome. Make as many birdies or pars or bogies depending on your skill level that you can, and have no conscience about it. Because in the metaphysical sense, golf does not care about you one bit.

I remember I was playing in the 1992 US Amateur at Murfield Village in Columbus, Ohio. I birdied two out of the first three holes in the medal rounds. I started on the back side and came to the short 14th hole two under par. I hit a beautiful tee shot. I was 74 yards from the pin, which ended up being too close to the green. I tried to hit my approach too close to the pin and flew the ball in the trap right behind the green. When I got to my ball, it was buried in the trap. I was so angry I ripped off my glove, smacked my leg and then made a triple bogey on the hole. I felt like my round was over after my fifth hole.

That thought process was absolutely ridiculous. I had 13 holes left, I was only one over par and I was hitting the ball really well. As I remember, there were not too many 65's that day. In fact, there were none. Even par would have been a great score. I lost my self-control because I was thinking too much of myself. I felt like I should have birdied the 14th just because I was so close to the green on my tee shot. Mr. Nicklaus built that hole especially for those folks like me.

After that round of golf, I was totally demoralized. I played terribly. I had never won anything in my life, but I fully intended to win the US Amateur, play in the Masters and US Open and then off to the tour. Instead of enjoying a major championship and all that went with it and not caring about how I played, I ruined my experience.

Irrational behavior comes from expectations that are misplaced in the mind. It is very rare that someone can control all parts of his or her mind and practice the tenets that we have discussed in this chapter. Playing better golf comes from good form and being in control or our ego. Patience gives us the opportunity to stay in the now and disregard our past and our future. Self-control will give us an opportunity to think rationally and make good decisions. If we play with joy, we can look forward to going to the golf course every day. Our outcomes will be much more acceptable no matter what the score. That is correct thinking, not crooked.

Lessons Learned:

- Crooked thinking is one of the main characteristics of poor play. Sometimes we have the ability physically, but our thought process gets in the way of our performance.
- Reactive sports sometimes are much easier because there is no time to think. Those of us that do not think and just do have an opportunity to keep things simple and less crooked in our minds.
- Our understanding of our game and ourselves must be challenged. It is very important to have good nature on the golf course. If we play happy we can play better.
- Learning to maintain self-control can help clear thinking. Allowing your anger to fester is not healthy. Use anger and frustration as a positive force for good play.
- Repressing anything causes pent up emotions that create other issues of insecurity.
- The best way to play golf is to make sound rational decisions over every shot. Making quality decisions is the model for any successful person.
- Patience is one of the key elements to being a very successful golfer. In competition or just playing for fun, those players that stay patient and in the moment will have a considerable advantage over others in the field.
- Do not think of your ending score until the card is signed. Scoreboard watching is for the back nine on Sunday only when you are in contention.
- By improving your nature, self-control, and your patience level, better golf, as well as better life, will be the result.

The caddy is receiving sound advice from the player.

V. Simplicity

"If you can't explain it simply, you do not understand it well enough."
-Albert Einstein

If something is complex and we try to make it simple, it does not always become easier. When we speak of the most difficult game ever played, we must understand that trying to explain something complex by referring to simplistic measures will only confuse and frustrate the performer. Many instructors in the game of golf, and other sports for that matter, try to obtain simple-minded explanations for application. This is mostly because they themselves do not understand the application process, so they try to make something simple by helping the student believe it is bad to think. Simplistic applications only work because the science that makes them work is usually present. For instance, if a player hits a ball next to the pin on an approach shot, that means that his club selection was correct for his particular distance, and this propels the ball toward the target. Simply put, the club face was looking at the target at the point of impact, and the ball was probably struck with power.

If a golf instructor stood in front of a student and said, "Keep your head still, make a big turn, and finish," and got the results he wanted from the student every time, there had to be other physical mechanical components involved for that explanation to work. If I could make a diagnosis about a swing with that simple terminology and explanation, there would be no need for golf to be the most over-taught game in history. It would be simpler, but I would be out of a job. That is why there are so many different ways to teach golf. Every student is an individual and every student has to identify with the information. One of the reasons that golf looks so simple on television is because the players are very talented. Talent and science are present in every player that plays at an expert level. Each player has an application process that is working for them, no matter what their score.

Even when trying to explain a good shot, I find myself reaching for an explanation that just cannot be given simply. It is like going to the doctor and trying to get him to explain how to treat you. It is not a simple explanation. In sports, education or anything for that matter, we have to come to a conclusion of how to make something complex easy to understand and apply. Therefore, we must use simplistic rudiments to do so, but understand that making things simple just to make them simple does not solve anything unless a concrete understanding is present.

Every day the sun shines, I take my eight-year-old to the golf course; I am amazed at his ability. It is not because he hits every shot the way that I want him to hit it; it is because he hits every shot until he is finished with the hole. I can remember one day in the fall he played nine holes on a par three course, and he scored very well. He made a couple of pars and a birdie. After the round, he decided he wanted to go to the regulation course and play. He played nine more holes. As I watched him, he played with no regard for score, ball hitting, putting or any other part of the game. The most enjoyable thing that I see is that he just plays what the game gives him. He disregards everything about the game that creates frustration or anxiety. He simply does not care about his outcomes. He wants to play every day. He does have the critical thinking skills to understand good and bad shots, but he just can't wait to hit the next one. He hits the ball, chases it until he puts it in the hole and then moves on to the next hole. Then afterwards, he wants to head to his favorite restaurant for pizza and lemonade.

We all want positive outcomes; therefore, we do need to be mindful of how we want to perform. But in order to be simplistic and efficient, we need to be mindful of the application process and understand that we cannot force outcome. My son gets feedback after every shot, but he always looks to finish the hole as the result. Many of us clutter our minds with so many different variables and negative aspects we cannot play. Just play the game. If you need a lesson on this concept, I can arrange some time with my son. His schedule is a bit cluttered, but I can get you an appointment.

Making something simple does not make it more efficient or more productive. We cannot just play the game and be satisfied with golf if we have specific goals that are unrealized. In many cases, the answers for this game can be realized by simple applications and experiences. However, getting there can take time. That is why we need to be structured in a way that highlights our capabilities.

I can remember a few years back having a detailed conversation with a sports psychologist. A gentleman I had worked with brought this fellow by for me to chat with because my student felt like I overemphasized mechanics. I was excited to talk with him because I have a high regard for sport psychologists. He went on to explain to me that we just need to "hit it, find it, and hit it again." Keep golf as simple as you can. His words were, "Just hit it." I sat with him for quite a while before I had to leave. I thought deeply about what we had talked about and tired to honestly process everything. His oversimplification could become detrimental to the learning process, which indeed can be a journey of enlightenment. "Hit it, find it, and hit it again" is a nice gesture if you have trouble with excess thought, but golfers need to experience a meaningful learning experience that has a baseline that allows them to improve.

One has to believe in a process, and let the process work. If you know your objective and give yourself the tools to perform, things can be simple. Any great player will tell you the best rounds of golf they ever played are the rounds that seemed easy. I can remember a fellow who shot a course record of 62. I asked the simplest question you could: "How did you do that?" He promptly said, "I made a five-footer on 18." How funny.

After I thought about it, I began to realize how profound his answer actually was. He claimed he shot the easiest 62 in the world. Everything was working. It was simple because he took advantage of a situation where his mechanics, his putting, his short game and his presence were all in tandem. He did not engineer any outcome. He saw his targets and let his process work. He may have thought about thousands of things, but that day he understood the things that worked. It was very obvious that he played in the now and did nothing to get in the way of his own success. We must understand that golf only becomes simple when preparation, experience and process are present.

Making something simple that is complex takes a real talent. I once had a professor of Philosophy and Religion in college who was so talented and intelligent that I wanted to take every class from him I could. He taught a course on Ethics at the university. The thing that made me so interested in the class was its subjectivity. I remember thinking, "Finally, a course with no answers." I was wrong. My professor brought us to concrete conclusions about very controversial topics. I began to see that the idea, "What does it mean to you?" did not really apply. Ethics was complex at the beginning, but the teacher made it simple because of his understanding of the subject.

Golf teachers often try to teach players, "What does it mean to you?" because they have limited answers themselves. I once had a teacher ask me during a lesson, "Now how did that feel?" I said, "The ball went 40 yards right, how you think it felt?" When asking someone how something feels you must be ready for the answers, because how something feels does not always contain truth. And truth is the simplest notion of all. In order to be truthful, one has to have command of the subject matter. The reason things look so easy when others do it is because of ability and preparation.

I was playing a collegiate event and I was paired with a gentleman who had the reputation of being a very good player. He had won his state amateur title a couple of times and several college tournaments. He also had the reputation of being a very boring player. He hit the ball down the middle not very far, hit his approaches in the middle of greens and made a lot of putts. I watched him beat me soundly for 18 holes. His game was so simple it was almost hypnotic. Every hit was straight. He putted well and chipped even better. The amazing thing was that he never changed his demeanor or expression the entire round.

This style of play seems very simple, but it is far from it. To achieve control over your emotions and your physical gifts is a challenge. It is really what separates those who play well and those who do not. This gentleman could not hit the ball far and did not hit the ball particularly solid all the time, but he played within his abilities and managed his game efficiently. I am always intrigued by a person with limited physical gifts who performs at high levels of competition. If we analyze different situations, many of the highest performers in our culture have overcome a great deal to become athletically, academically or occupationally superior. So how do we teach that?

One of things I have heard a lot in my career is that you can't teach talent. When I think about that statement I sometimes wonder if that is true. Can someone be taught to be talented? I am sure we cannot teach a 300 pound man to be a race horse jockey, but I think you can cultivate the talent in every individual regardless of their athleticism, physical build or intelligence. The teacher just has to figure out how to do it. This is where we should find the simplest of answers to every problem. Talent is all relative and it is in the eye of the person trying to define their personal objectives. The simplistic approach to any task is to define the objective. We all need to define what we want, and be specific. Most people lack the primary personality trait that is necessary to be great, which is commitment. Total commitment is a fleeting characteristic of most human beings. Most people lack the courage to commit and find it very difficult.

The great players commit. After commitment is established, a huge emotional burden is lifted. Things become less debilitating because we have made a decision to dedicate our self. Those who commit are not afraid of being wrong or failing. Those who have never done anything wrong or failed have never achieved. A good friend of mine gave me a wonderful little phrase I use often. "I am often wrong, but I am never in doubt." I have always been in awe of great golfers, great athletes and very successful business people. How are they so sure of themselves? They simply believe this little phrase.

Those of us who doubt will never accomplish anything. The disciple Thomas is a great example. Thomas was a very intelligent and thoughtful man, and maybe even a relative of Jesus. He never acted without principle. He was not a hasty thinker, but he lacked commitment in the belief that Jesus was the Messiah, forever labeling him "Doubting Thomas." Lacking commitment means lacking conviction, which leads to limited belief. And with no belief comes confusion. As for hitting golf shots, every time we step to the ball, we have to be committed. We have to commit to our swing and most importantly our decisions. Commitment makes things simple. It relieves the stress of indecisiveness.

Indecisiveness brings about a plethora of unwanted psychological thoughts and emotional feelings. It drains us physically. Stress breaks down our nervous system. Being indecisive creates stress because it is the unknown. The unknown confuses us and creates fear. This is why it is so difficult to teach great players of any sport. Many great players do not understand what they do. They just do, so when you teach them, if they do not understand they withdraw from the teacher. To teach a great player, first examine his or her spirit or, in today's terminology, heart, and understand that talent is secondary. If someone has no decisive commitment, they have a limited chance of achieving anything they desire. They will surely struggle on the golf course. A former heavyweight champion once told me that, "The jails are full of better fighters than me." The best way to teach talent is to help a player commit to a process and a system that fits their environment and their talent. Not every player can do the same thing.

People do not usually fail, systems fail. For instance, properly diagnosing a swing flaw is not easy. The trick is to analyze someone's swing and prioritize certain aspects, but at the same time explain why their ball is going where it is going. If the explanation is correct and the player has a clear understanding of it, successful outcomes are usually present. I have been around several good players that say they just want to keep things as simple as possible, but they do not realize how they complicate matters by not knowing.

Conversely, most amateurs make excuses about instruction because they fail to understand how difficult golf really is. I once had a student tell me that he was ready to work on his game. His wife had to be out of town for two weeks so he was going to work every day on his golf game. We were going to change everything. He told me that he was either going to swing properly or he was not going to play again. This should have been a big red light for me since there really is no proper way to swing, the swing variables just have to match. I told him we were going to fix his left arm alignment and his weight distribution first. This guy moved all over the ball, and what made it worse was that his left arm alignment was straight up and down. We tried to get his left arm a little more inside on the backswing and tried to stabilize his weight shift.

The first round of golf he played after our lesson was pretty good. There were no catastrophes. The second round was a different story. I asked after the second round how he played and he blurted out, "I am never going to use that flat swing again." He never came back for another lesson, and he never got any better. Lesson learned for him is to never let his wife go out of town again. The lesson for me was to never try to teach someone who thinks he knows more than you do.

Obviously this man lacked a clear understanding of how difficult golf really is and had no idea what it takes to be a better player. Most amateurs look for that simple solution. Contrary to many golf publications, you cannot think the ball in the hole. Golf is a game of application and process, whether it be physical or psychological. Simple application does exist, but as we said before, structure also has to exist. Most folks just lack the will to stick with anything long enough to make a difference.

Take physical fitness for example. If you are overweight, eat less and exercise. Most people can't do that. They cannot get off the couch, walk a mile, sit down on the floor to stretch and stop overeating. They want to be able to take a diet pill, eat whatever they want and get in shape. Most of us lack the simple discipline it takes to make positive changes in our lives.

Discipline is another characteristic that you will find in most great players. I define discipline as an ability to resist laziness and to repeat activities that help us improve. If I am trying to correct my swing, I should have the discipline to practice that motion every time. I should ignore my target results until I have seen the visual picture change. If I have made the proper change and my results do not change, then I have incorrectly diagnosed the problem. I then have to have the discipline to start over and continue working hard until I achieve the results I want.

This is a key ingredient of the world's best players. I do not know Tiger Woods, but I have observed that he has changed his swing often. Why? He thinks he can always get better is my guess. The thing that makes Tiger so fantastic is his discipline. I never have seen a player with his determination. It is extraordinary. Every shot has a purpose. Even though he is physically gifted, he has seriousness about his practice that makes playing easy. Not everyone has the ability or the desire to be great. Most everyone would like to play better golf if they could, but are they willing to do what it takes to become what they really want. Most of do not know what we really want and that is very troubling. That is when we become very unhappy in life.

The determination one establishes to be a better player starts with the notion of simple ideas. Simple ideas come with not so simple applications. The key to making golf an easier game is to make sure that your application process is functional, and your commitment and discipline to that application process are working. We all love things that are simplistic. However, what we all find to be most gratifying is when we doing something that is difficult, make it look easy and get what we want.

Lessons Learned:

- The simplistic approach to golf starts with understanding the basic principle of playing the game.
- Do not complicate the game with overanalyzing. However, do not oversimplify the game because you will lose your ability to think critically and you will create unforced errors.
- Critical thinking does not have to be complicated; in fact, critical thinking is sometimes more simplistic.
- Do not allow your results to interfere with your goals. The smart player will use experience to achieve desired results.
- A good player learns to establish the commitment necessary to make positive changes or maintain successful results.
- Playing and practice discipline is a trademark of simple play. The more discipline a player projects the more complete that player will be.
- Be determined. This will remove doubt that complicates all the bad process that we encounter. Do not guess. There are concrete answers for swinging, thinking, and management.

Mason at four years old. We started early.

VI. Respect Not Fear

"The fear of the Lord is the beginning of knowledge; but fools despise wisdom and discipline."
-Proverbs

The one emotional state that keeps all of us from reaching the pinnacle of our success is fear. Fear is paralyzing. It makes us irrational, insecure and creates unimportant thought. I have always wondered why one person with the same ability as another does not succeed while the other does. I believe those people suffer from fear. Those who are afraid will always get less out of their ability than those who are not. There are very few people in life that are willing to confront their fear and overcome it.

What causes fear? The behaviorist John Watson was the first psychologist to link fear to learned behavior. He believed that fear was a learned component of one's environment. Our environment plays an extreme role in our development. It is one of the great influences on human behavior. In this instance, we are not speaking of the environment in the sense of the outdoors, even though our physical environment can have a profound effect on our learning, but rather the places, people and information that shape our experiences.

Golfers tend to allow their games to be created by their environment. It influences how they think and feel on the golf course. If a junior golfer grows up playing a lot of golf in Florida and is constantly faced with water hazard after water hazard, he or she becomes immune to the perception that water is something to fear. Those players that play more links-style courses where water is less likely to come into play may have a different perception when playing in competition. Our environment raises our awareness of stimuli that exist in our immediate surroundings.

Who we associate with can also have a very positive influence on our personal, professional and athletic lives. This is why Jesus commanded his disciples to be in a community of faith. He taught that being among a group of believers was essential to spreading His massage of grace. Those people in our environment that have the biggest impact on our life are our family, friends, teachers and coaches. Throughout my career, I have tried very hard to be a wise teacher, as well as someone who can help create a positive and productive learning atmosphere. Wisdom is tied to decision-making and action. It is very important to be a wise thinker, but at the same time the individual has to learn to incorporate wisdom through experience.

Many people that create a positive environment for their habits usually do pretty well. Some players find hard work and intensity fun, and others just want to be entertained. The wise teacher knows the difference. I had a very dear friend of mine tell me once to give people what they can handle. Sometimes people do not want to know what you do. We have to ask ourselves are we doing it for them or are we doing it for us. That is something I ask myself daily when I am interacting with my children. I want my children to get out of life wonderful things, but do I want it for me or do I want it for them? It is a very interesting question. In a productive environment, there needs to be people present that can lend support and nourishment.

We also need people to push us and help us learn how to be competitive. The key ingredient to a competitive environment is establishing the core reasons for the competition. One of the reasons the United States is so overwhelmingly successful compared to the rest of the world is because we are competitive. We create competition in our market place and then compete for commerce. The same concept applies to our golf game. We must learn how to be competitive in our environment and enjoy the competition. Embracing competition makes us better. We should be fearful of competition. We should love it.

Competition is the biggest contributor to comfort and security. The better competition we have, the better player we will become. If we play competitions on easy golf courses, we have to make sure that the caliber of player is such that under par will be a leading contender for the tournament win. In today's competitive junior golf world, under par is a common score. Juniors are literally playing 20 weeks out of the year and traveling thousands of miles to play. Juniors are becoming so comfortable under par just because that is what it takes to win. The earlier we learn to score low, the better player we will be as an adult.

Conversely, the best way to learn is to play the most difficult courses and conditions all the time. It teaches many things, most importantly mental toughness and shot making. The harder the golf course, the more comfortable we get with scoring. On difficult golf courses, our perception constantly changes. We learn to deal with difficult shots for sure, but we are constantly dealing with the anxiety and perception issues that go with playing difficult holes. Longer shots over difficult terrain force players to get emotionally comfortable. Another good boxing analogy is the more rounds you fight, the less you worry about getting hit. If you are constantly worrying about getting knocked out, you never look to your offense. Your opponent paralyzes you.

The same applies on the golf course. If players are constantly challenged by uncomfortable shots, it taxes the nervous system. Eventually, we wear out physically, mentally and emotionally if we are not conditioned. We see this constantly in the major championships. The environment just plays havoc on the minds of the players. The only way to overcome those conditions is through experience. All players must condition themselves to deal with the most challenging of golfing paralytics. If your environment is filled with nurturing people, positive information, good experiences and rewarding stimuli that give you feedback, fear becomes less debilitating.

A friend of mine was playing in a local two-man tournament recently when his golf course panic attacks reared their ugly head. It was a team competition, one best ball of the two. His team was easily favored to win because he and his partner were very strong players. The first hole of the day my friend hit a decent tee shot that cut across the corner of a fairway bunker on a par five. This got him a little closer to the green and actually allowed a good chance to get the ball close to the hole. He selected his club and hit a wonderful shot right on target. The ball came to rest on the green just 10 feet underneath the hole. He had the opportunity to have a great start to the event. His partner hit his second shot just right of the green and pitched to about 12 feet right on the same putting line. He hit his putt first and made it. He carded a four.

The team had the birdie; now it was time for my friend to step up and make the putt for eagle. He knew the break because it was on the direct same line as his partner's. The putt was uphill and if he missed there was no pressure because they already had a four. Surveying the putt, he began to feel the pressure of making this putt. He could not stop thinking about the results before they happened. Then, all at once, another insane thought came into his head: "You need to open your stance a little more to control your speed." What? He missed the putt low, short and left. That was the only place you could NOT hit the putt in order to make it. After missing the putt, the tone was set for the day.

As we analyzed the situation, we realized that he didn't putt for many eagles. Therefore, he became self-conscious about his score and talked himself out of the putt because he was afraid of missing. An eagle is a bonus on the score card. It is an infamous score related to powerful second shots on par five holes that lead to scores under par. We know this subconsciously, so many of us are always aware of our score when we have unique scoring opportunities. That is one of the first mistakes players make because it terrifies some golfers into playing under par. Fear causes us to relay destructive self-talk. In order to eliminate fear in our environment, we must focus on the here and now. It never matters what we have done, but only what we are doing.

Another key to evaluating fear is analyzing our exposure. I have a particular student who is from a small rural town with very limited golf facilities. This particular student is very talented, but he lacks exposure to facilities that challenge his game. Because of rural upbringing, his golfing development has been a bit slower than we both would like it to be. When he approaches very difficult driving holes with water or other intimidating obstacles, he lacks the confidence to hit the shot he is capable of because he does not encounter many of those intimidating holes at his home course. There may be other factors that are driving his fear, but what I understand from him is that he is not used to hitting those particular shots and is afraid to hit his driver unless the holes are wide open. He told me he can hit shot after shot in practice, but in practice there are no consequences. As I came to find out after a little more probing, he does not drive the ball that well when he plays his own course. There were no obstacles in the way so he does not hit many fairways. His consciousness knows this when he is playing a tough golf course. We are consciously very perceptive. We innately pay attention to ourselves more than we think. His environment in this case has taught him that he is not a very good driver of the golf ball. He knows this and is afraid to hit his drive on a big golf course with lots of trouble, because even on his home course he does not drive the ball well.

It does not matter where you grow up as long as the elements for growing are fertile. You can be from High Society Country Club or Gravel Stitch Municipal. The key is to understand what it takes to play well and spend a lot of time outside a comfortable environment when you practice. Simply put, don't play your home course all the time. Play courses and hit shots that you have trouble with when you are practicing.

I would make this young man play on my course instead of his and hit shot after shot with his driver on the course to eliminate his fearful approach to driving. I would film him on the course and show him how his swing was working. I continued to reinforce my approval until he overcame all his anxious tendencies when he approached the tee box. I was essentially "blowing up" his perception. He had learned his behavior from countless practices on the course where he grew up. He learned there were no consequences for poor shot making; therefore, his confidence and his decision-making were skewed in the direction of fear, anxiety and indecision. In order for him to overcome his fearful nature, he will have to spend hours practicing in an environment that is not reinforcing his poor play. The ultimate test will come in competition.

If he can overcome the playing field and learn to be confident outside of his current comfort zone, there is a real chance that he can become a very good player.

One of the core components of how we react and interpret situations and people is based on our value programming. We all have particular emotions and thoughts about how things should or should not be. Political ideology, religious beliefs or just plain core values help explain our actions and our circumstances. When we experience situations outside our value system, we immediately have a fear of the consequences. Our values play a tremendous role in our daily lives. Values do not have to be a moral standard or statements of purpose. Values do not necessarily come with any definitions. Value programming may or may not be recognized by the individual.

Growing up, my family and I always opened presents on Christmas Day, never Christmas Eve. There are many families that open presents on Christmas Eve, and reserved Christmas Day for Santa's gifts. I have strong feelings about presents on Christmas Day, only because I had been programmed for 20 years to think that opening Christmas gifts before Christmas morning was just wrong. Different sets of values may require additional flexibility.

Just imagine how value programming can have an impact in other areas of our lives. Can you imagine how our values affect monetary purchases, relationships or religious affiliations? Imagine what it would be like to make a decision on doing your duty if you were a soldier? It is a good thing we are just talking about golf or we could spend hours discussing just this topic alone.

Most of our decisions come with no personal awareness. We just know that the feelings and thoughts are present, and we have no idea why we do the things we do much of the time. Fear is a learned behavior. We fear what conflicts with the values we have learned.

Gambling on the golf course is a great way to train yourself to be mentally tough, especially if you play for more money than you can afford. Playing for a little money always makes the competition a little different. When I was coming up in the competitive ranks, I had a friend who was always getting me into money games. He used to tell me it would increase my toughness and get me ready to deal with the pressure of tournament play. My value programming did not allow me to feel comfortable playing for money because I thought gambling was wrong. I was reared with the simple notion that money was hard to come by and should not be gambled. Gambling interfered with my programming and made me feel differently on the golf course. I could not focus on the game. I could only focus on the money being wagered. That was not quite the reinforcement I wanted, but it did teach me how to deal with my emotions in a different way on the course.

I would make adjustments that I normally would not make just to keep from losing my money. There was one thing for sure: Playing for a little money made things a whole lot more complicated. As I have grown older, I have come to understand those emotions and now prefer to play for money. Perhaps I have become morally bankrupt with age, or maybe I feel like I now have a little cash I can lose. At any rate, I am much more comfortable now because of my training. But again, our values play an interesting role in our process. If our values are compromised, we will be afraid.

Our golfing values are identified when we decide to play golf in certain groups, competitions or just for leisure. If we grow up where competition is encouraged, then we are much more likely to embrace the competitive nature of sports and overcome any fear of competition that we recognize when playing. Competition becomes fun instead of a stressful and unwanted situation. Value programming plays a critical role in how we display our emotions.

Our temperament on the golf course can be fierce. It can be detrimental to how we play. Sometimes we are so competitive that anything less than a pure shot or a made putt is virtually unacceptable. I used to embarrass my parents and friends on a regular basis because of my lack of control. I had been programmed to not accept anything unless it was absolutely right. If I ever played poorly, I could not recover for several hours. For years, I asked myself why. Now I understand: My desire to be better and different made failure a very scary thing and nearly drove me to rage every time. My programming was so severe that I could not possibly succeed or, more importantly, have any fun.

Being one of the only young guys playing gave me the identification that I needed. It made me feel special and different. That was positive in some ways, but negative in others. If I played poorly, it was a devastating blow to my ego. It is very important to answer self-directed questions. Anger usually ends up being fear. Apprehension also is an indicator of fear. Those fears are usually displaced by a lack of confidence and especially faith.

Fear is something that everyone has encountered. Fear can cause a variety of different actions or reactions. We become very irrational when we become fearful. Irrationality becomes apparent when we lose control of a clear thinking process. Being irrational is something that happens to us all, but especially when we become aware of all the things in our environment that cause us anxiety.

Golfers, especially, are irrational thinkers. They become plagued by fear over the silliest things. I once had a lesson with a lady who proclaimed she was afraid to play in competitions because she did not want people to think badly of her. She was so petrified about her tournament performance that she could not bear the idea of someone else thinking she was a bad golfer. Obviously this lady had some self-image problems.

What did we do to fix this irrational belief? First, I changed her belief system by firmly explaining to her how ridiculous her paradigm was. In order to combat irrationality, you have to confront it with facts. The second strategy I used was risky. I insisted that this lady play in the club tournaments. I would not take no for an answer. Even though she never was an expert player, or even an average player, she approached the game of golf with a fervor that allowed her to enjoy her friends more, make new friends and accomplish some other goals along the way.

I tell my children frequently about the difference between respect and fear. Fear will keep them from getting what they want out of life. Even though my youngest is very young, I want him to recognize the difference. Respect means that you have a genuine regard, whether it be psychologically or emotionally, for someone or something that you encounter in your environment. We talk quite a bit about the idea of fear-based paradigms. Respect is quite different. One can be respectful and temperate, but not afraid.

Your approach to the game of golf can be linked to the same explanation. If you have to carry a water hazard by 280 yards and decide that laying up is the way to go, I would say that you are respecting the course instead of being afraid of the course. Respect for your own ability also has to be mentioned. If you are not a long hitter, do not try long hitter shots. These are good judgments, not fear.

Being afraid will cause the greatest to become weak, but understanding our fears and confronting them can awake a potential within us all that produces results. These results can be life-altering. When King David confronted Goliath, he stepped toward him with no fear and slung the rock. The giant fell. We all have Goliaths in our lives. We must arm ourselves with a fearless spirit that respects our obstacles, but does not allow them to overcome our desires.

Disregarding fear is not our objective. We want to recognize what makes us feel fear and think about it until we are aware of our self and our circumstance. It is always in our best interest to confront our fears and make sure they do not dominate our thoughts and feelings. In order for us to confront our fears, we have to have an honest dialogue with ourselves as soon as possible, because lingering fear only allows for more perilous golf play. An affirmation of courage and belief will allow us all to move forward. We must understand that we are all afraid of failures and not realizing dreams. The only thing worse than being afraid all the time is looking back and thinking how much we regret not ever taking the chances that made sense. Everything needs clarity and perspective. Fear is only a lack of knowledge and faith. Respect fear, but do not give in to it.

Lessons Learned:

- Fear is one of the main reasons we never attain our desires and goals.
- Fear is a learned behavior that is influenced by our environment and those in our environment who have an impact on our lives.
- Our value systems will have a great influence on what we deem acceptable and true. If we have conflict with our values we will fear outcomes that may or may not be what we truly want to accomplish.
- We fear what we do not understand. It is imperative that we gain important knowledge that will help us grow and overcome those situations that we are uncomfortable with and begin to install a belief system that fosters comfort and courage.
- All of use struggle with issues of self-esteem and self-image. Self-image and self-esteem have a well-defined impact on all of our lives and will certainly drive us to the brink of self-destruction if we allow ourselves to be over influenced especially by what other people think. We must remember that we need to be our own biggest fan.
- Fear produces irrational thought patterns that we are totally un-aware of at times. Being irrational can only be overcome if the student is willing to understand how to best deal with fears and anxiety at the times that are the most important. Always remember that regret is one of the most awful and damaging feelings that we can carry in our psyche. The emotional toll that regret takes on our souls is a damaging consequence that can be very difficult to deal with. Understand your fears and confront them.

Mason after his first win, chatting with Bill Moore, PGA Professional

VII. The Mind and the Self

"So the single most vital step on your journey toward enlightenment is this: learn to disidentify from your mind. Every time you create a gap in the stream of mind, the light of your consciousness grows stronger."
-Eckhart Tolle

There are thousands of expert or proficient golfers in the world. These golfers include professional players who tour the US and around the world, club professionals, collegiate players who compete in amateur ranks and amateur players that compete in tournaments at a par or better level. The most talented, obviously, are those who compete on the US PGA Tour.

Next are the handicap amateur players. These are the people that play some competitive or club golf. They play the game for fun and recreation. There are tens of thousands of these folks. So what makes some players better than others? Can it be athleticism? I cannot believe that is completely true. We have seen many great athletes unable to hit a golf ball with consistency. What makes the difference?

Obviously proper swing mechanics do produce better golf shots. The game is certainly not completely mental; in fact, it may be much more physical. There is definitive empirical evidence pertaining to a well-executed golf stroke and the results we can glean from that particular stroke. When calculating the proper stroke pattern, you have to realize that there cannot be any conflicting variables. For instance, the face angle of the club cannot be open to the target line in hopes of hitting the ball at the target if the path angle of the club is swinging across the ball. These are basic, physical geometric facts. No matter what any swing teacher might say, the ball will only go where the clubface leads it as it relates to the swing path of the club.

One defining characteristic of great golfers has to be supreme confidence. How do these people get that inner view of themselves that makes them feel so sure of themselves? I believe it is an inward confidence and a reinforced awareness of the self.

It's related to what modern psychologists define as self-esteem. Self-esteem is the conception that one has of oneself, including an assessment of qualities and personal self-worth. Self-esteem is a feeling of personal pride and value. It is a defining point for human beings because it allows us to combat fear, personal insecurity and depression. Golf can be a very stressful game, especially when it's competitive. Feeling a sense of power about your self is invaluable when it comes to any type of individual performance. Self-esteem enhances confidence.

As with most things, self-esteem can be reinforced by events or people. There could be research that suggests our neurology predisposes us with certain personality traits that allow us to possess self-esteem without reinforcement. However, I believe that our behavior patterns are mostly learned; therefore, reinforcement becomes a form of learning.

Most of us can think back in time and name certain events that helped develop paradigms about how we feel about our ability to perform. Recognition of positive events helps to build self-esteem. Individuals that experience these patterns of achievement can expect self-esteem to develop at a rapid pace. This is a contagious condition: the more positive the reinforcement, the more feelings of self-worth. So when we discuss why some players are better than others, when the physical gifts are comparable, we can point to life experiences that led to positive self-esteem development.

This would be especially true in childhood. We develop a great deal of our power as individuals when we are children. That is why it is so important for children to have positive experiences in a nurturing environment. There are exceptional children in life that overcome obstacles in a very negative environment and do not have positive experiences. They are the fighters in life. Somewhere along the road, these kids experienced a sense of empowerment that made them tough and resilient. However, a positive and nurturing environment creates more opportunity for stability.

Single events tend not to define the thoughts and feelings children have toward themselves if some form of nurturing is present. Negative experiences need to be accompanied by a clear explanation of positive reinforcement by a loving and nurturing person, whether it is a parent, coach or friend. If children can establish self-esteem at a young age, then those attributes should follow into adulthood. If these positive thoughts and feelings about the self are present and are accompanied by humility, the definitions we have about ourselves are clear. Other opinions tend not to matter to us. Those individuals who are very successful almost never allow any one person to define them. That type of emotional and psychological strength will prove to be a great ally, especially when playing golf.

However, as with any good advice, we must keep everything in context. We still need to listen to people that are close to us: parents, teachers, coaches, friends, ministers, spouses or even children, if these people have our sincere interest in mind. We need to continue being aware that we are not the only people in our environment.

But the best part of being successful is having a deep understanding and confidence in yourself. We do not need to confuse confidence with conceit. We also do not want to confuse our self with our thoughts. Our thoughts are not necessarily who we are. I do not agree with the saying, "I think therefore, I am." Eckhart Tolle, a well-known spiritual teacher, teaches that we need to not identify our self with our mind. Our minds can use us in ways that creates all kinds of turmoil. If we fall victim to our thinking, especially if that thinking is compulsive, our self becomes weakened. We have to separate the self from the mind, and make sure the thinking tools we use are a healthy.

How do we know if they are healthy? We will be happy, clear, peaceful and, most of all, able to express love. This is the true relationship between the mind and the body. Thinking is essential in any task. But as Tolle says, our minds are merely a tool that needs to be put up when we are finished. Someone who does not think is merely expressing a lack of experience, maturity or maybe both. It is what and how we think that is important. Rancid thinking, whether it be in daily living or on the golf course, breaks down self-esteem. Therefore, it is important to understand that your mind, that produces thought, is not necessarily a definition of who you are as a person. Inner peace must be the focus.

There are many words used to describe a peaceful heart. Buddhists call it enlightenment, Christians call it grace and many psychologists refer to it as self-actualization or existentialism. Whatever definitions we use to define peace and enhance our self-esteem, know that reinforcement from events and others are helpful, as well as a deep feeling of accomplishment.

In the movie *The Last Samurai*, there is a scene where the main character is practicing his swordsmanship. He is struggling with his practice so one of the instructors gives him the advice of "No Mind." He asks the student to just not think and then his mind will be clear. It is how we think and process that allows us to perform. If we just do, our thinking becomes peaceful. If we analyze, doubt, render something to difficult or fight against improvement, we will become bitter and frustrated.

That is why "No Mind" is important and why we have to disassociate ourselves from our thoughts. Because we are not what we think; we are what we do. Jesus said something very profound and important in his teachings. It does not do any man any good to know lofty words or phrases. A man is measured by what he does.

Should we stop thinking? No. However, we need to understand that the essence of who we are is separate from our thoughts, and we need to use our thoughts as tools to increase our self-esteem that helps us bear fruit. We then can add value to the self.

Lessons Learned:

- Those players who come to the golf course with high elements of self-esteem will exhibit decisiveness and control. They will play with confidence and assuredness. The outcomes will be much less frightening.
- We all know that when things are going our way we tend to be much more comfortable than when things are not going our way. It is the mark of a true winner when the stressors of life are barring down and we can overcome what has caused us the most pain.
- We must remember more winners in life are made than are born.
- Self-esteem can be taught by parents, teachers, friends or even our own self-talk. We just have to listen.
- As individuals, we must subscribe to an ideal about ourselves that is positive and reinforcing.
- Most people would rather see us lose to cover their own imperfections or unhappiness. So we might as well believe in ourselves and reinforce the good stuff.
- Listen to those individuals who care about you personally, but always understand that we must possess an inner toughness that creates a belief in ourselves.
- We are separate from our own thought. Thoughts are tools that we may use to enhance our abilities. Strive to find the inner self that creates peace, harmony and growth in our spirit.
- We all have a spirit that is capable of wonderful things. We can evaluate our spirit mentally, but if we are still and really listen we can understand what is really important in life and how we can move forward with clarity.

Clay's parents, Tom and Sandra Hamrick

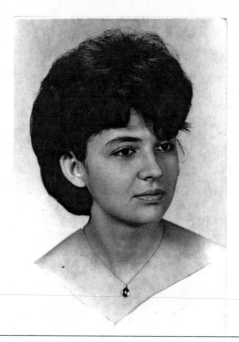

VIII. Pressure

"Success depends upon previous preparation, and without such preparation there is sure to be failure."
-Confucius

We all define pressure differently. The way we do has a lot to do with our personality characteristics, our self-esteem and our environmental exposures. Those who have trouble under self-defined pressure usually suffer from self-esteem issues that tell them how awful it would be if they do not live up to the task. Those folks that deal with pressure the best only see the task at hand and never think about the consequences of not executing. Pressure is relative. It is totally dependent on the attention we give it.

Feeling pressure is the result of lack of preparation, exposure and paradigms. There are some very bad phrases that we use in our mind. "I must" and "I should" and "I have to" and "I need to." These little phrases create a great deal of unconscious and conscious barriers that turn into stress. The way to deal with anxiety is to identify the stress and use some very basic tools that will provide coping mechanisms. When we use these tools, we will actually enjoy pressure moments and be better adjusted when we experience stressful environments.

First, get prepared. Preparation is key in dealing with pressure impact situations. Preparation can overcome many anxieties. Our preparation can be as simple as saying a prayer, relaxation techniques or studying. Being a good golfer comes down to your ability to deal with pressure. Having an understanding of our individual preparation needs allows us to become comfortable with what the game offers us on the golf course.

Any weaknesses that an individual player has will be exposed on the golf course tenfold if that individual is not prepared for the shot at hand. Being unprepared for a particular shot or situation disrupts our comfort. Comfort zone is used to describe the level of psychological, emotional and physical comfort an athlete has in his or her environment when they are performing their athletic activity. If you are playing a round of golf and find yourself three or four under par, and then suddenly become nervous about your score and make a double bogey, you could determine you were out of your comfort zone.

The term comfort zone is a personal label, and it is very dangerous psychologically to label ourselves. Comfort zone can be used to excuse underachieving. We can use our comfort levels as a crutch if we feel like we did not get what we wanted. The problem with recognizing comfort zones is it creates limitations on performance. Our personal comfort zone is ever expanding. It certainly is not a constant. Our comfort zone can be changed with each experience we encounter. This is why preparation is so important. Preparation is an individual assessment of what we may think and feel about our performance tasks. Preparation has everything to do with expanding that comfort zone in order to deal with situations that create anxiety.

The second way to deal with pressure is to define your paradigms. Definitions are very important. They give us a baseline or a foundation for examining performance. If the definitions about our individual needs are so severe and beyond our capabilities, the pressure we have put on ourselves is very difficult to overcome. Pressure is usually self-designated unless you have a psychotic or maladjusted parent, spouse or coach. By analyzing your paradigms, you have the opportunity to see if the pressure put on yourself is downright silly or not enough.

Pressure can be a contributing factor to your success on the golf course or it can be a detriment. It is all about how you define yourself and your game. Some people work very hard to try to be something they cannot be. They do it for other people or reasons other than personal betterment and usually end up making themselves a nervous wreck. I once heard the story of a young tour player who was very talented, but was miserable on the golf course because his father wanted him to perform at a certain level at such a young age. This boy felt like he could not measure up to the expectations that were put upon him. He obviously struggled.

Unfortunately, this runs rampant in today's families who think their child is going to end up on the cover of *Sports Illustrated*. This lack of understanding from parent to child is truly sickening. In order for this young man to play and enjoy the game, he had to be enthusiastic about what he wanted to do, not what his father or anyone else wanted him to do. This young man finally turned his career around and became very successful. But it was only because his father was not involved. There is a fine line between pushing your children and shoving them over a cliff.

In order to compete and enjoy what we are doing on the golf course, we all have to define parameters. This idea applies from children to high handicap players to even the tour player. If you feel your golf game is inadequate, some part of your game will not work. We all can leap from inadequacy to higher levels of golfing performance; however, we have to prepare and have defining paradigms in our games that allow us to make that leap. If our definitions are not compatible with our capabilities and our preparation, there is great potential for struggle.

The third and most important practice of dealing with pressure is also the most obvious: experience. Experience is paramount to dealing with pressure. The more times you put yourself under pressure and execute, the more likely you are to make pressure your ally. If we expose ourselves to an environment filled with pressure over and over again, that experience will eventually be minimized to where we actually miss having that feeling when it is not there.

I can remember playing in many pressure-packed events with definitive goals in my mind and meeting them. It was a rush of unbelievable satisfaction. After playing with all that pressure, the game became easy. My father went with me to caddy in an amateur tournament on one occasion. I needed to make one more birdie to qualify for the event. I knew what I needed to do and I was thriving on the pressure. I looked toward my dad and said, "I love this." I had finally played enough golf to feel good in this environment. That was my best summer playing golf. If we put ourselves under pressure enough, it will eventually become our greatest weapon. We must remember that pressure is not the enemy. We do not need to neutralize it; we need to understand it and deal with it.

There is a difference between stress and pressure. Stress is debilitating and can make us sick. Stress does not have a particular focus. Pressure does not have to be stressful and is often times relished by the performer. We do not want to make pressure impact situations cliché or dismiss them. Pressure is relative to the performer. Just as a friend of mine who was in the military said, "I've been shot at; golf shots are not that big of a deal." Again, pressure is relative. It is theologically wrong to say that the truth is in the eye of the beholder and that perception is reality all of the time. But when it comes to pressure, you can be playing in the US Open or a Sunday Nassau and feel the same. Embrace pressure by showing each situation attention and use the tools you have been given. Do not ignore your feelings. You either spend your time exposing yourself to difficult situations, or you take no risk and stay right where you are. If you fail, you at least gain an opportunity to learn and figure it out at another time.

Another tool that lies within us all is our imagination. We all have an imagination that has no limit. Our imagination can conjure just about anything we allow. It puts us in places that let us rehearse situations time and time again. Every aspect of teaching can use imagination to increase learning capability. Proper use of mental imagery can identify with our desires and give us feedback through our feelings. That is why a lot of counseling therapy deals with how we feel. Carl Rogers, a well known counseling psychologist used a client centered format to help people recognize their own thoughts and feelings. This type of therapy helped his clients realize their own neurosis that lead them to a powerful form of learning. This is exactly how our imaginations can work to our benefit. Imagery, when used correctly, involves the application of rehearsed images that aid performance. Our imaginations can empower us to be in constant learning mode. All we have to do is identify what we need to work on and be specific. However, imagery without the proper specifics is just day dreaming.

For example, one of the true sins of the golf swing is what golf teachers call "casting" the club. Casting, or what I call throwing the club away is a dreadful problem. Casting is where a student will allow the club and their arms to get into a straight line on the downswing too soon before impact. Imagine the club coming down from the top of the backswing. The wrist starts to break too soon and the club eventually hits the ground before the club hits the ball. Explaining that concept over and over again to a student can be difficult to grasp. The student must be able to feel the change physically and understand the change mentally. So the goal is to find a mental image that allows the student to change the application during the swing.

The problem with casting is that all golfers think about accumulating power. When someone has this swing ailment, accumulation of power is a killer because their feeling of power is coming from the throwing motion. In this instance, imagery is an effective tool. The instructor must help the student understand the best image to get the club down to impact without throwing the club away. The instructor must also have the diagnostic process in place for the solution to work. Once the instructor understands the process, the student must understand the application mentally and physically. Mental imagery and a healthy imagination can be a great ally.

Most of our stress is self-induced, and everyone reacts differently to stress. What stresses me out may not bother you. I am so envious of those people who do not let the little things get to them. Using a vivid imagination often helps with the reduction of anxiety.

I am not a flyer. I cannot stand airplanes and probably will never feel comfortable up in the air. I am sure it has something to do with my controlling nature, but I don't care. I simply hate flying. It makes me sick, uncomfortable, nervous and just downright mean. I also hate driving long distances in a car, so that makes flying a necessary evil when I have to travel long distances. My imagination is very vivid on a plane, mainly because I am scared to death. I like to think of happy times in my life when I am 30,000 feet in the air. Maybe these good images become apparent when I fly because subconsciously I am terrified and my good thoughts become defensive. After all, you become very existential when you feel like you're about to perish. We all have things we are uncomfortable with, whether we want to admit them or not. Flying for me is tough. It is liberating for others. That is the great thing about being individuals. I can remember a student of mine who had a golf phobia that is equal to my irrational feelings about flight.

This gentleman had trouble with long iron shots. He constantly thought about "shanking" the ball. It is just like that airplane. When I walk onto the plane, I instantly got nervous. When he drew the three-iron out the bag, he immediately thought, "SHANK!" I fixed most of the mechanical flaws in his swing, so he did not shank the ball very often. But for some reason he still let that thought enter into his head when he used long irons. There have been many times, especially in competition, he had to stop himself and start over because he was thinking of shanking the ball. So what did we do to get rid of the thoughts that manifested into feelings every time he pulled a long iron out of his bag? First, I explained what caused the shank so he understood what was causing the shot, and then we imagined him using his wedge swing every time he hit a three-iron. It worked!! All we had to do was find something that worked for him. It was very simple, but also very effective.

We have mentioned the effects self-esteem has on our performance many times. However, we have not given self-image equal time. These two conditions are very different. Self-image deals with the feelings we have about ourselves concerning what others think of us. We base our feelings on how we view other people's perception of us. Self-image is a determination of one's own view of the self. If I am playing golf, why would I worry about hitting a bad shot unless I cared what someone else thought? This is the reason for first tee jitters. The amount of self-talk that goes on in our thoughts on the first tee is truly the devil's playground.

Self-image issues can be debilitating and distract us from performing at peak levels. We are so fixated on what others might think that we lose track of our objective. Self-image problems stem from learned behavior patterns because the ego is trying to either please or impress. This is due to a lack of security of the individual in their own mind. We said before the self is not the mind. The mind can be a tool used for destruction or for enlightenment. In order for us to combat self-image issues, let us return to the childlike tendencies that can teach us all how to be healthy adults.

As children, we are very powerful psychologically. We see images of ourselves that make us feel invulnerable. One of the true tragedies about the human condition is that we allow other people and events in our lives to destroy all that power deep within us. If we do not produce the results that we desire or we feel like people do not like us, we harbor those images and let them shape our lives. I am not advocating childlike behaviors as an adult, but what I do advocate is childlike dreaming.

Imagery is at its most powerful state when individuals can see their dream and work toward a way to make it happen. Walt Disney's motto was, "If you can dream it, you can do it." Every time I walk into Disney World, I am reminded of the dreams that make us truly free in our minds and in our hearts. Golfers need to carry that image to the golf course and see themselves accomplishing wonders instead of worrying about outcomes. Whether it is winning a big tournament by making the final putt or hitting the longest tee shot of your life, it is the childlike dreams that place our spirit in a place that brings about total joy. We have to remember the dreams in our heart and imagine being in a place where you can see them fulfilled. I guarantee you will be satisfied with what you receive.

Proper use of imagination is an ingredient to becoming a very good player. Our imagination can enhance our ability to prepare, help us define self-enhancing paradigms and make our experiences something we learn from the rest of our lives. The pressures of life can be tough. We need to embrace pressure and learn from it, and only then will we welcome the opportunity to compete on its biggest stage. Avoiding pressure will not do any of us any service. We will never truly realize what we are capable of until we have an understanding of what it means to achieve something that is difficult.

It is very fulfilling to accomplish something that we have dreamed about for years. The tools are at our disposal. All we have to do is choose to play.

However, there is one ingredient left that has to be present in order to make all of this happen: Work. All great genius in life has been accompanied by hard work. Michelangelo once said, "If the people knew how hard I had to work to gain my mastery, it wouldn't seem wonderful at all." The journey in life is what is important. That is why we continue to emphasize the present and the now. Hard work has to accompany us on that journey because accomplishment brings fulfillment. If a person realizes how hard they worked at something and got what they wanted, their accomplishments in life are much sweeter.

Hard work is also very healthy. It creates a rhythm in life that satisfies the appetite of the dream. A broad sense of accomplishment creates a foundation for unlimited growth. Those that wait on life to offer what they want without working for it will be waiting a long time. That is why so many people who inherit wealth or win the lottery end up broke because they did not labor for what they earned and have no appreciation for what they have. That may be why Jesus said it is easier for a camel to go through the eye of a needle than for a rich man to inherit the kingdom of heaven. There is nothing wrong with the accumulation of things, such as money, titles, education or property, but it is how we get those things that make a difference.

I am convinced that God wants all people to live happily and with abundance, but we must recognize how we get there. Laziness is a deadly condition. Pressurized moments in life will devour the lazy and unprepared. Every professional athlete that achieves on a championship level is always recognized as a tireless worker. If we analyze the careers of all great achievers in life, hard work is central to their accomplishment.

We have two choices in life: Eat or be eaten. It is all up to us. If we choose to let the stresses of life keep us in despair; that is our choice. If we let situations or other people dictate to us that we are unhappy, that is our choice. True joy only comes from within. Other people are not responsible for how we feel. We have total control of our outlook on life. Pressure and stress are relative to the individual. We have to define what certain things mean to us as individuals and give them due attention. If we ignore anxiety, we will certainly struggle with pressure our entire lives.

We have tools at our disposal that allow us cope with life's stressors. It is how we use them that are important. We must possess courage as individuals and take calculated risks that allow us to live life to our fullest measurement. Work hard, prepare, dream, experience and don't label yourself. You will win.

Lessons Learned:

- How we handle pressure can play a vital role in playing better golf. It can separate the tour player from the tour winner, the mini-tour player from the tour player and the high handicapper from the low handicapper.
- Remember that pressure is all relative on every level of competitive or recreational golf. How we deal with that pressure is a key to achieving the desired success that we all want.
- We never want to discount pressure or act as if it is not there. We want to recognize it and use it to our advantage so we eventually welcome the challenge and miss those wonderful pressure situations that have the opportunity to make us successful.
- How do we do we turn pressure into something we want? First we prepare. We hit the proper amount of practice balls; we putt, we chip and play. After preparation we define our paradigms so we can lay out clear definitions for purposeful play.
- We have to realize that we are playing for ourselves because we love to play and it is a fun way to spend our lives.
- After clear definitions are established, we now need the necessary experience to compete in a Sunday foursome or a competitive tournament.
- The golfing experience has to be repeated over and over again until the pressure we feel actually feels good. Remember that we will come to enjoy playing under pressure because under pressure success creates more feelings of accomplishment than any other part of competitive success on any level.

Clay's children, Mason and Mary Clay

IX. Redemption

"People are often unreasonable and self-centered. Forgive them anyway. If you are kind, people may accuse you of ulterior motives. Be kind anyway. If you are honest, people may cheat you. Be honest anyway. If you find happiness, people may be jealous. Be happy anyway. The good you do today may be forgotten tomorrow. Do good anyway. Give the world the best you have, and it may never be enough. Give it your best anyway. For you see, in the end, it is between you and God. It was never between you and them anyway."
-Mother Teresa

The most powerful state of the human condition is forgiveness. Not only do we need forgiveness as it concerns others, but, more importantly, we need forgiveness for ourselves. There are times when we fall short of our own expectations. How we deal with those times is very important for our development and our progress. If we choose not to forgive others and ourselves, we will continue in a quandary of emotional resentment. Redemption is a new life. When things go wrong, starting over is powerful. Those who live in a state of constant regret will never experience life to its fullest capacity. Nothing about man or man's experience is perfect. The notion of perfection is truly a fool's notion.

One could ascertain that the game of golf is all about redemption. Every shot is a new beginning. Every hole is a new adventure. Every game is different. The conditions change, the relationships change and certainly we change with every experience. When the game is analyzed from every nuance, it is a wonder that anyone can play it well. Imagine if we could not get past a poor shot, a missed two-footer, a ball in the water on the last hole or the collapse of the entire game when you are in contention.

Very rarely do I like to mention anyone by name, but I have to mention Greg Norman. Greg Norman is and was one of the premier players of all time. He sustained a level of golfing excellence for a tremendous period of time and he defined how the modern game is played. Norman's record will always be chastised. . His collapse at

Augusta in 1986, 1996 and the US Open loss at Shinnecock will always be remembered rather than this man's unbelievable world record.

Can you imagine what he had to endure, not just from others, but in his own heart? If Norman did not forgive himself and move forward, he would have never played at the level he achieved. For that, he has to be recognized as one of the great sportsmen of our generation. The demons in his head had to be there for years, but you would never know it. I do not know this man and probably will never know him, but to me, he has had to endure the most trauma of any single great player in the history of golf. I do not think Norman could have played if he had not felt a sense of forgiveness for his unfortunate happenings. We measure records in wins and losses. In Norman's case, if we measured wins by sheer emotional endurance, he would surely be worth 20 majors.

For forgiveness to work in our hearts, we have to believe in it and be sincere. Sincerity is everlasting. When we find a sincere person, we are drawn to him or her. We have nothing but good things to say in their regard, brag about their character and want to be around them. Why not become that person to yourself? Illuminate your own mind and heart, and become the light of sincerity that you admire in others.

I remember playing in a US Open Sectional Qualifier when I was 18 years old. I was extremely nervous and felt like I was trying to accomplish something that was just not possible. One of the guys I was playing with was a pretty good player. With every shot he hit, I practically became a speechwriter for him. "Oh nice shot, great play, way to go!" My dad was caddying for me at the time, and he pulled me over to the side and said, "You are making me sick complimenting this guy. Play your own game and stop cheerleading."

My father has said many true statements in his life, but this was one of the truest. My sincerities should have been directed at myself rather than my playing partners. I am not saying that I should not be sincere with my playing partners or not be courteous, but I should certainly give myself the same regard. Being good to yourself makes it easier to be good to others, no matter what you are doing.

It is much easier to play golf when there is no additional baggage. Someone who is playing with thoughts other than the game at hand has already accumulated two to three shots on the field. It is obvious when people carry psychological baggage. We create our own "junk bags." I have no patience for someone who is unwilling to empty his or her bag and start over. This is the epitome of self-indulgence. These people are saying, "Look at me, my life is so terrible," or as it relates to golf, "My game is so terrible, and I do not deserve this."

For those players who do not accept forgiveness, you might as well quit. You will never get beyond where you are. The best players in the world are very forgiving to themselves. They hit bad shots and move on. They do not think about what happened, only what is going to happen. Add up your scorecard and head to the range. Moving forward is a primary mechanism for leaving the past where it belongs: in the past.

Undoubtedly, children are the primary example of what it means to forgive. My young son plays golf with no worries. I can fuss at his play or his behavior; he will get upset, cry and then forget about it 30 seconds later. That is why the good book says not only to forgive, but also to forget. You must forgive and forget in order to truly redeem and absolve yourself of any misgivings. Moving on without any regard for the past is essential when playing golf. Think of the emotional scars that are left by thinking about what could have been: Anger, frustration, regret and even remorse. We can only learn from past happenings; we can never change them.

Absolving yourself is very important. Being freed from our mistakes gives us a second, third and fourth chance. It is perpetual freedom from self-tyranny. In a game as unrelenting as golf, being able to dust yourself off and move on is a primary weapon against hating the game. It is hard to love something when it constantly reminds you that you are inadequate and inferior.

Everyone must remember that golf is the hardest game that has ever been played. There is no mastery of it, only a sense of temperance. The only true way to approach the game is to understand that it must be respected and observed. So to truly be compatible with the game, be a proponent of forgiveness and forget your mistakes or misgivings you made when playing. This will save you the awkwardness of trying to be perfect.

Redemption is a powerful tool. Being able to start over is an important part of organizing our emotions. Golf is the perfect sport for doing just that. Each shot should be looked at as a new beginning. There is a chance at redemption on each particular play throughout the game. For those who struggle with the emotional and psychological part of the game, there is a good chance they do not want to be forgiven for mistakes on the course. If these people were examined thoroughly, this would likely be a consistent theme in their individual lives as well.

The way to forgive yourself for meaningless circumstances like golf shots is to understand the importance of what we are all trying to accomplish. I am not one to ignore the passions that people have in life for occupation and/or recreational dreams. I also am not one to say that it is just a game. A game of golf can be a defining opportunity for someone's emotional or psychological well being, as well as a very lucrative financial occurrence. However, context is important. We cannot relate anything we do in life, as far as our occupational or recreational activities go, to who we actually are as a person. If we feel like we have failed, we only have to offer ourselves a proper understanding of that failure and look forward to the next experience with optimism. Those of us who bury ourselves in the abyss of self-pity will linger there for most of our days.

Failure is a part of success, maybe the biggest part. Look for the new, and learn from the old. Forgive and forget. Your golf will be much better. Like the Proverbs say, "Blessed is the man whose sin is forgiven and covered up."

Lessons Learned:

- Redemption is a powerful state of emotional and psychological well-being.
- Forgive and forget poor shot making or outcomes. Forgiveness leads to spiritual freedom. If we do not forgive the spirit is in constant conflict with the mind and the actions we display in daily living. An unforgiving heart produces destructive behaviors.
- All action has to be dealt with according to context. It helps us evaluate the true meaning of what we try to accomplish in our lives.
- One of the key ingredients of redemption is the acceptance of the outcomes and the acceptance of the forgiveness.
- We all fall short. The one who can forgive will always have an outlook on life that recognizes a change to grow and a change to learn.

Clay's sister Marnie Burress and her family: Husband Richard, sons Nathan and Dane

X. Transcendence

"All reason and natural investigation ought to follow faith, not to precede, nor to break it. For faith and love do here especially take the highest place, and work in hidden ways in this most holy and exceeding excellent Sacrament. God who is eternal and incomprehensible, and of infinite power, doth great and inscrutable things in heaven and in earth, and His wonderful works are past finding out. If the works of God were of such sort that they might easily be comprehended by human reason, they should no longer be called wonderful or unspeakable."
-Thomas á Kempis

As a finale to this commentary, how do we transcend into the player or person we would like to be? I have always been told that you can tell a great deal about a person by playing a round of golf with them. I am not sure that I agree totally in principle with that idea, but golf is a good indicator of how we think and sometimes behave. Anytime we offer a certain amount of seriousness to an occasion, we will come to understand a great deal about our character. Let's examine the game in a sense of how it reflects upon our ability to be a better golfer and relate it to our ability to be a better person.

Certainly the first step to becoming a better golfer or person is recognizing something we need to work on as an individual in order to grow. Being a better player and person is necessary in order to evolve and stay healthy emotionally, psychologically and physically. We have to recognize that we are not always in the place where we need to be. This is awareness. Simply stated, getting better is good. We also need to own up to the fact that we are all flawed. Sometimes that is difficult to admit. If we reach the point in life where we recognize that we have to make changes in order to progress and we cannot do it ourselves, we then have to turn to other people.

Given the awkward nature of confessing we need help, it is only natural to assume that coaching is a necessary and vital necessity to any relationship, whether it is a team atmosphere or individual situation. Sometimes it takes a while to get to this place in your golf game or your life. We must seek God first and then his miracles will be abundant in our lives. Then we seek out the teacher, counselor or friend that will help with the transcendence of your situation, because people are the hands of God. There is a very old Zen saying that indicates when the student is ready, the teacher will appear.

Coaching and teaching always need to be present in life as well as any sport. We play the game individually, but we must rely on a team of people to help through the tough times. We all must think clearly to understand our personal challenges and look in the mirror each and every day. Even though we have mirrors, do they really allow us to see ourselves? Sometimes it takes others to give us an indication of how we act.

I have found through the years that many of the best golfers in life are very self-aware. That trait can be essential to becoming a great player. Without it, we will lack confidence, the ability to make accurate decisions and eventually make mistakes because of our indecisiveness. Being self-aware allows us to understand that we are the most important person in the arena at that time, and nothing else really matters.

However, there is a dichotomy here. That is what it takes to be a great player, but does this notion apply to being a great person? One of the reasons great athletes fail personally with the public is because they are so self-absorbed. The general public gives them a tremendous amount of power and usually they take it. Professional golfers are indeed no exception. Even though being self-aware is necessary to be great on the course, arrogance can lead to being to self-absorbed in life and can certainly lead to problems. When people stop taking responsibility for their own behavior and reach a sense of entitlement in their own mind, a breakdown will be eminent.

A condition of spiritual presence needs to be in our lives, along with a community of sincere supporters that helps us make the proper decisions because we cannot do it alone. I had a great teacher who happened to be a caddy once tell me, "I can see the things that you cannot." That is extremely profound. That is the entire reason the golfer will always need to have the teacher.

When taking instruction, recognize that you need to learn something. Education for the sake of participation is not education at all. Education or learning has to be meaningful. It has to be interpreted by the learner as significant. If a powerful learning opportunity presents itself to the student, then desirable change will take place.

This form of learning is what the great psychologist, Abraham Maslow, called self-actualization. Maslow believed that all human beings possess intrinsic values of dynamic individualism. His approach to psychology and learning was very humanistic and dealt with the capacity of individuals to be self-fulfilled. Much like the Greek Philosopher Aristotle's self-realization, Maslow highlighted the individual's ability to experience growth through forms of meaningful experiences along with creativity and choice that promote psychological and emotional health. Maslow notes that self-respect and the feeling of being accepted and loved by others are all essential conditions for mental health. If these conditions are present, meaningful learning takes hold and self-actualization occurs. Maslow notes that these people are not burdened with conflict or debilitating conditions of anxiety. They are what the Buddhist would call enlightened.

This does not mean that these individuals are free from frustration. In fact, it is not the nature of positive learning situations to be free from frustrating experiences and certainly not desired. Those individuals who have experienced meaningful learning can overcome frustration easier and react with healthy solutions.

I can remember years ago having my golf swing completely together for about three weeks. I was able to hit every shot. Scoring was easy. I physically understood my swing. I would move one thing, and the ball would just fly. Long, straight, beautiful, powerful and majestic. Magical things were happening. I went to the range everyday and practiced the same thing over and over again.

I can remember vividly one afternoon on the practice range when I lost my swing. Since I had experienced such success in the previous days, I thought it was just a matter of time before it came back to me. But it never did. I struggled for six weeks. I never hit the ball the same. Even though I was playing well, I really did not know why. I thought I had experienced sufficient learning, but I now realize I did not. If I had cataloged my stroke pattern, I would have known exactly how to fix my swing and play better.

The most powerful component of learning (Maslow would agree) is experience. Indeed, one of the key ingredients of meaningful, transcendent growth is putting yourself in a position to gain experiences that will help you understand processes that are trying to be learned. Growth opportunities need to be filled with positive and reassuring events that lead to nourishing experiences. Most things are simplistic; it is people who make them complex.

A nourishing golf experience allows the golfer to understand what has occurred, whether it is information or accomplishment, and then execute the process over and over again. Experience entails a tremendous amount of failure. It is often said that someone who does not fail does not try; therefore, failing is a critical element in gaining the necessary ingredients for a meaningful and successful experience. The key to understanding failure is how we deal with it and how we define it.

Nothing to me is more sickening than to hear someone constantly lament on the failings of the day. Everyone fails. It is how we see our failures that determine our state of mind. Here is some good advice if we fail: DO IT AGAIN! Keep trying. If we want to be accomplished and transcend into the person we want to become, we need to follow some very simple steps. These simplistic steps are as easy as determining what we truly want out of our lives.

We usually have one opportunity in life to do what we want. First, we must determine what we want, which for many of us is a huge undertaking. The reason why this is such a difficult task is because many of us are not decision makers. I have come across countless individuals that have no ability to make personal decisions about their basic wants. Wanting something is an important part of making a decision about the existential variables in our lives. Those wants can be monetary, occupational, recreational, emotional or just as basic as choosing what to eat for the day. It becomes very frustrating to deal with an individual who does not know what they want. Usually that means they are selfish, but other times it can be an indication of other factors that are much more severe.

Being indecisive kills the confidence mechanisms in our psyche. Even if you are wrong about something, never be in doubt. Commitment is a major issue for many of us. I have found people that get the most out of life are not committed all the time, but they are decisive. Change is a necessary part of learning. Change is transcendent because it is recognition and that can be attributed to learning.

We all certainly want to get what we want out of life. Defining the want is very important. I wanted to be a professional player. I have now come to understand that I really never wanted to be a professional player at all because I did not do the things necessary to become that player. My defining paradigms were self-defeating.

I would challenge anyone to reflect that much about themselves and reach a conclusion, or just sort out some ideas about the truth concerning their individual golf game or their life. Can you have an honest conversation with yourself about your abilities and about the things you are thinking and feeling?

I hope that all people want to improve. Getting better is self-defining at times, but any type of individually defined improvement is healthy. Improvement implies a state of well being that is nourishing to the mind, heart, body and spirit. The pursuit of knowledge and, more importantly, truth will allow us all the ultimate opportunity to become better people.

As for the game of golf, much is still not known about this great sporting enigma. Golf is the most difficult simple game in the history of sports. I often wonder why it is so popular. I do believe that golf is popular because it can be played by the very worst player and the very best. Golf can also be classified as a culture. It is appreciated by those who are mesmerized by the honor and fairness that the sport represents. There is indeed not another sport that provides such individual dignity in its rules and in its play. Being a lady and a gentleman is synonymous with being a golfer.

I hopefully have given you all an opportunity to see this game in a different light and help you understand that we are all individuals who have taken many different paths, but are trying to end up at the same place.

Golf is truly something special. Golf provides an intense motivation for sports, as well as a much-needed social and physical outlet for individuals, families and businesses. If we are going to play golf, why not understand how to play better and also understand a little about ourselves along the way? We will never figure the game out completely, but we must identify the truth about the game. In order to be good or better at anything, we all must subscribe to set of principles, bound in what is good, that will transcend all that we wish to accomplish.

We are all defined by what we believe. If we believe in nothing, we are indeed empty and everything that we stand for is fleeting and will not last. It is important to subscribe to a set of profound principles about yourself and your golf game, believe in them and commit. That is why a spiritual faith ground in the Grace of Almighty God will instill in us a foundation for a happy life. We will never fully conquer our lives or golf for many reasons. But we must continue to have faith, believe in our abilities and continue to pursue that which is important to us.

Faith and love are the most powerful components of the human heart. God exists in all things small and great. It is through Him that nature and heaven will be granted life and accomplishment. I said early on that no amount of wishing, thinking or any other form of cognitive powers will make your ball go where you want it to go if you have a faulty technique. That is all true. However, a spiritual faith and a loving heart will put your mind in a place that gives you an opportunity to reap the proverbial wheat that you have sown.

Golf is a game that is special in many ways. If it were readily understandable or explainable by human reason, it would neither be wonderful or special.

Lessons Learned:

- In order to transcend the spirit, first recognize the need to be a better player and a better person. After we recognize that there is a need for growth, we will undertake a whole new procedure for our lives. We will recognize we have more to learn and more to give.
- Do not judge others before judging yourself. Look for the planks in your own eye not someone else. This will give you an understanding that we all are the same and have equitable gifts.
- Maintaining something great is very difficult. Never be completely satisfied, but always understand that maintaining greatness is a rarity.
- There will always be a need for each one of us to be taught. How we are taught is special to that individual.
- Being self-aware is very important, but do not allow yourself to become paranoid about your performance. Your awareness needs to enhance your performance in a positive manner not in a way that creates restrictions.
- We will never be free from frustration. The path to true enlightenment and peace is the manner in which deal with the most unpleasant things life has to offer. We all will experience loss in life, but it is how we deal with our loss that is the mark of a true champion.

"My Son, I the Lord am a stronghold in the day of trouble. Come unto Me, when it is not well with thee."

Clay's Acknowledgments

When we sit and think of all the people who have touched our lives and what they mean to us, the list can be long. I have dedicated this book to four very special people, my parents and my children. However, there are people outside of these four who have had a profound influence on my career and my personal life.

First, I must thank and acknowledge Don McNay who saw in me a talent and saw in this book an opportunity. Don is not only a good friend, but also a partner. I by nature can be very indecisive. I analyze things at times to a fault. This is not Don. He saw an opportunity with the book and decided immediately to publish it. Thanks to Don for giving me the much needed push in life to become something I always wanted to be, which is an author.

Every man should have spiritual advisors. Those people can be lay or professional people. In my case, I have always relied on the most professional and academic of spiritual teachers. Currently, Dr. Glenn Birkett, Senior Minister of First Christian Church, Richmond KY, is my Sheppard. His wisdom and depth of religiosity has given me tremendous insight into many of the questions I have as a Christian and a thinker. Dr. Tom Greener, quite possibly the most considerate and passionate individual I have ever met about matters of faith, was instrumental in my growth as a person of faith. Dr. Greener is not only a very good golfer, he is an amazing intellect. He is certainly the epitome of what it means to be a minster of the church. Dr. John C. Cooper, who is deceased, is a man who changed my life. He helped me understand what it means to be a man of God.

Andy Plummer was my college teammate at Eastern Kentucky University. He began to develop his concepts about the Stack and Tilt Golf Swing system during his collegiate days. After many years of research, development and trial and error, Andy was gracious enough to include me in many of his swing insights. He certainly showed me the truth as it relates to hitting a golf ball. These notions have led me to many of my thoughts concerning how the game of golf can be played and taught. Thanks to Plum for the help.

Lew Smither II was and is my Golf Coach. Lew is not only an intelligent and wise man, but was a tremendous teacher of young men. I cannot thank Lew enough for the opportunity he gave me to play in college and pursue a career as a golf professional. I attended Eastern Kentucky University because of Lew, played golf because of Lew and became a golf professional in large part because of Lew. Every young man should have the opportunity to spend five minutes with this man. I am very fortunate to have spent several years with him.

A true gentleman by the name of Harlan Piatt started me playing golf as a boy. He never charged me a penny. I never knew this. Harlan was like a grandfather to me and will live in my heart forever. He was a tremendous man with so much to offer a young boy who did not want to do anything except hit golf balls. I grew up in a small farm town in Southern Ohio. We only had a nine-hole course with no practice area. Harlan and I would hit balls into an open field day after day. Those days were indeed special.

There are two golf professionals who have had a profound influence on my career. These gentlemen were my first and my last boss. Jon Tatersol, a Golf Instructor from Atlanta, GA taught me the difference between coaching and teaching. His cerebral approach to managing golf instruction is second to none. I am so pleased to have been in his company for so many years. I have truly only had one business mentor in my career and that is Billy Peterson. Billy instilled in me a confidence that was much needed for my personal growth as a business professional. I was very fortunate to have the opportunity to spend a year with Billy under his tutelage.

I have never been the principal instructor of a top tour professional. However, there is one young man, besides my own son, who has given me more pleasure than anyone could give me as it relates to teaching and playing golf. That young man is Marshall Pickett. I started teaching Marshall when he was eight years old. He has unlimited ability. I have watched Marshall grow and develop his game, and I hope he continues to follow his dream of being a tour professional. I would like to thank Ron and Cindy Pickett for being

109

such a big part of my family. They are indeed special.

Dr. Robert Adams was the chair of the Psychology Department at Eastern Kentucky University when I attended. Dr. Adams not only spurred in me a profound interest in sport psychology, he helped me create a foundation academically that allowed me to develop my current notions concerning sports and cognition. His simplistic approach to thinking was vital to my development as a student and athlete.

JWT....Thank you for everything as you know what you have done to help me.

It goes without saying that there is one person that has my best interest at heart at all times. That is my sister Marnie Burress. I am so proud of Marnie and her family. She is impressive on so many levels it is hard to imagine. She and her husband Richard and their two precious boys, Nathan and Dane, are a special family. Thanks to them for being such a loving part of my life.

I would like to take this opportunity to thank Matt White and Ernie Hobbie for being such strong father figures to me.

Glen Jones, Doug Flynn, Dr. Tom Martin, Robert Gooch, Ken Haigler, Dr. Richard Cummings, Brain Hayes, Jim Farley, Jim Yonkers, Bozie Tart and Kent Clark are men who have helped shape me in many ways. I would like to thank my Uncle Dave Tomlin for bringing me so much joy as a child. These men have showed a special interest in me and for that I thank them.

I have the most amazing family. I have four aunts, Sharon Ann, Sonya, Trudy and Zina who have served as a surrogate for my deceased mother. Even though my mother could never be replaced these four women have been nothing but a pure blessing to me. I also want to acknowledge the remaining members of my father and mother's family as well as all my teammates, friends and confidants, which are many. As well as a wonderful lady who is no longer with us, Thelma Anderson.

And of course David E.

The *Life Lessons from the Golf Course* team:
Don McNay, Anne Parton, Clay Hamrick and Adam Turner

Don's Acknowledgments

"People you've got the power over what we do
You can sit there and wait
Or you can pull us through"
-Jackson Browne

Along with Clay Hamrick, two key people made this book happen:
Anne Parton and Adam Turner.

Anne Parton is Director of Operations for McNay Consulting. She
coordinated the writing of this book, contributed several key ideas,
supervised the editing and promotion process and organized many
aspects of my business and my life. She also interviewed Clay
Hamrick before I agreed to work with him and coordinated my golf
lessons. She is bright, insightful, intensely loyal and the ultimate
professional.

Adam Turner, Editor and Multimedia Guru for McNay Consulting,
edited, designed and did the layout on this book, just like he did with
the bestseller, *Life Lessons from the Lottery*. He is bright, incredibly
pleasant, with a great work ethic and a bright future.

An interesting thing happened to my wife, Karen Thomas McNay.
Three months after we were married, a headhunter called out of the
blue. A few months later, she accepted the position as President of
the Ursuline Academy in New Orleans.

At 285 years old, the Ursuline Academy is the oldest Catholic school
in the United States and the oldest all girls' school in the United
States. I am going to commute from Kentucky to New Orleans, but
Karen is intensely scouting out golf courses for me in the New
Orleans area. I am very proud of her.

Karen is loyal, loving, intuitive and extremely intelligent. Growing
up on a dairy farm, she is not afraid of hard work and has the perfect
temperament to be married to a husband with multiple careers, who

works long hours and took up an obsession with golf, which she does not play.

I adopted my daughters, Gena Bigler and Angela Luhys, after they were adults. Angela brought me my first grandchild, Abijah Luhys. Gena and her husband Clay brought Adelaide and Liam into my life. Both Gena and Angela have leadership roles at the McNay Group (**www.mcnay.com**), and Clay serves as company president. Some people hire a great organization. I adopted one and love them dearly.

Gena started writing a very popular "smart money" column for KYForward.com, under the tutelage of legendary editor Judy Clabes. Another aspiring writer in my family is my stepdaughter, Emily Kirby. Her and her brothers Max and Zach joined my life when I married Karen.

I write about Al Smith in this book and dedicated my last book to him. He and his wife Martha Helen need to be acknowledged every book for their love, loyalty and being wonderful role models for how life should be lived.

I've been fortunate to befriend some of the best writers in America such as Gary Rivlin, Ed McClanahan, Byron Crawford, Dave Astor, Judy and Gene Clabes, Bill Robinson, Jack Brammer, Tom Eblen, Suzette Martinez Standring, Al Cross, Samantha Swindler, and Rick Robinson. Joe Nocera, opinion page editor for the *New York Times*, has been a great friend and mentor. He did a wonderful column about my *Life Lessons from the Lottery* book in December 2012 and another a couple of months later, about going to a gun range, where my daughter Gena Bigler, taught him how to shoot.

From the broadcast world, Renee Shaw, Kelly Wallingford, Dave Baker, Ferrell Wellman, Jim LaBarbara, Joe Elliott, Tom Leach, Neil Middleton and Keith Yarber are friends whom I admire and learn from.

I've attempted to shorten the acknowledgements but the following people deserve a shout out in making this effort happen: Peter

Perlman, Mike Behler, David Grise, Bob Babbage, Lee Gentry, David Grandgeorge, Jerry and Margie Parton, Pierce Hamblin, Robb Jones, Bill Garmer, Kevin Osborne, Andy Kaiser, Mike "Sid" Glockner, Steve O Brien, Larry Doker, Donna Davis, Ivan "Buzz" Beltz, Tom Sweeney, Shelia Holdt, Richard Hay, Randy Campbell, Debbie Fickett-Wilbar, Sam Davies, Linda Davies, Samuel Davies, Laura Babbage, Keen Babbage, Stephenie Steitzer, Len Press, Lil Press, Yvonne Yelton, Nancy and Paul Collins, Connie Kreyling, Bill Walters, Crystal Hamblin, Nicole Gilliam, Kaye Spalding Peterson, Carroll and Janice Crouch, Dr. Phil and Nancy Hoffman, Luke Martinez, Adam Collins, Harry and Kerrie Moberly, Dr. Skip Daugherty, Wes Browne, Sydney Napier Thigpen, Father Ronald Ketteler, Father Richard Watson, Phil Taliaferro, Joe Greathouse, Hans Poppe, Gary Hillerich and Len Blonder.

My wife's favorite film is *It's a Wonderful Life*, and the last line of the movie is, "No one is poor who has friends."

By that standard, I am rich beyond all measure.

Clay Hamrick, PGA Professional

Clay Hamrick is a PGA Professional from Richmond, Kentucky, and General Manager at Battlefield Golf Club. Clay attended Eastern Kentucky University, where he completed a MA of Arts in Counseling Therapy, a BS in Psychology and minored in Religion Studies. He also is currently an adjunct professor at Eastern Kentucky University.

Clay has been a Golf Professional for 17 years. He has gained an extensive teaching and playing background during his career, giving nearly 15,000 individual golf lessons since his career began in Wilmington, North Carolina. Clay is considered a true student of the game. He has taught all ranges of golfers from the professional to the beginner. His extensive knowledge of the swing mechanics have given him tremendous insight into the game of golf, as well as enhanced his ability to understand the mentality necessary to become a better player. Through thoughtful observation, Clay has been able to offer some insights into how golfers can learn the game through a process that allows them to develop structural practices that they can practice and measure.

Clay first became interested in writing when he felt like there was a void in golf instruction as it related to how players get better. He soon understood that golf, like our very own lives, encompasses a variety of different learning tactics and experiences. Clay noticed that golf is an over taught game and most people do not get better when they play and practice. That is when he sought to try to link life experiences and playing the game together in order to bring clarity to the individual player. Through his training as a counselor, his playing and teaching background and countless hours of study about spiritual matters, Clay has managed to touch upon some interesting concepts that will allow the reader to understand how they may get a little better playing golf and at the same time learn a little about themselves along the way. Information is only useful if the person receiving the information applies the principles.

Clay is an amateur theologian who is well versed in early Christian Church Doctrine and is also well versed in other world religions and their practices. He practices Christianity and is a member and deacon of the First Christian Church, Disciples of Christ; Richmond, Kentucky. He is also a very accomplished musician.

Don McNay, CLU, ChFC, MSFS, CSSC
Best-Selling Author, Syndicated Columnist, Financial Consultant
www.donmcnay.com

Don McNay, a financial consultant and award-winning writer, is an expert on managing money and one of the world's leading authorities on how lottery winners handle their winnings.

His syndicated financial column appears regularly in *The Huffington Post* and in hundreds of publication worldwide. McNay also has appeared in several hundred television and radio programs, including *CBS Morning News, CBS Evening News with Katie Couric, ABC News Radio, BBC News, KPCC- Los Angeles, WLW-AM-Cincinnati, Al Jazeera-English, CBC Television* (Canada), *CTV* (Canada) and *Radio Live* (New Zealand).

His insight has been sought by hundreds of print publications, including the *New York Times, Los Angeles Times, Chicago Tribune, Reuters, Associated Press, USA Today* and *Forbes*.

McNay has written four previous books. *Life Lessons from the Lottery, Wealth Without Wall Street* and *Son of a Son of a Gambler: Winners, Losers and What to Do When You Win the Lottery* have been number one Amazon bestsellers in a number of business and investing related categories.

Entering the financial services business in 1982, McNay was a pioneer in the field of structured settlements, helping injury victims and lottery winners handle large sums of money.

He founded McNay Settlement Group Inc., which is part of the McNay Group (www.mcnay.com). The organization is considered one of the world's leading experts concerning structured settlements, mass torts and qualified settlement funds. His company has been noted for its work with special-needs children, along with injury victims and lottery winners.

A graduate of Eastern Kentucky University, McNay was inducted into the Eastern Kentucky University Hall of Distinguished Alumni in 1998. McNay has a master's degree from Vanderbilt University and a second masters in Financial Services from the American College in Bryn Mawr, Pennsylvania.

McNay is a Lifetime and Quarter Century Member of the Million Dollar Round Table signifying that McNay met the organization's highly selective standards for service, production and ethical behavior in 25 different years.

McNay has four professional designations in the financial services field.

Don received the Certified Structured Settlement Consultant (CSSC) designation from a program affiliated with Notre Dame University. He is a Chartered Life Underwriter (CLU), a Chartered Financial Consultant (ChFC) and earned the Masters of Financial Services (MSFS) designation.

In 2000, McNay helped found the Kentucky Guardianship

Administrators, which administers qualified settlement funds nationwide and serves as a court-appointed conservator for juveniles and incapacitated people. He is the owner of McNay Consulting, which provides advice for business owners. McNay is a fee-based insurance consultant for individuals and businesses in Kentucky and a licensed claims adjuster.

Among his professional involvements are former Treasurer of the National Society of Newspaper Columnists and former Director of the National Structured Settlement Trade Association. He has spoken numerous times at structured settlement industry conventions.

McNay has won several awards for his newspaper column, including "Best Columnist" from the Kentucky Press Association.

Don is a former Director of the Eastern Kentucky University National Alumni Association and served on the Advisory Council for the Eastern Kentucky University College of Business. He was named Outstanding Young Lexingtonian in 1985 by the Lexington Jaycees. He is an honorary Kentucky Colonel and named as an honorary Duke of Hazard by the Mayor of Hazard, Kentucky. He was in the initial group of people named to Legacy Society at Eastern Kentucky University and has served on the University's Planned Giving Committee. McNay is a University Fellow at Eastern Kentucky University and a University Fellow at the University of Kentucky.

McNay created the Ollie and Theresa McNay Endowed Memorial Scholarship at the Eastern Kentucky University College of Nursing after the death of his mother and sister in 2006.

A prolific author and lecturer, McNay has spoken to hundreds of legal and financial groups throughout the United States, Canada and Bermuda. He has published research articles in *Trial*, *Round the Table* (the official publication of the Million Dollar Round Table,) *Claims Magazine*, *Best's Review*, *Trial Diplomacy Journal*, *National Underwriter* and other financial industry publications.

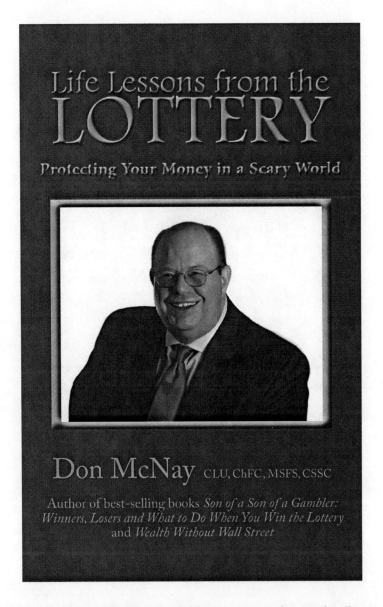

Life Lessons from the
LOTTERY

Protecting Your Money in a Scary World

Don McNay CLU, ChFC, MSFS, CSSC

Author of best-selling books *Son of a Son of a Gambler:
Winners, Losers and What to Do When You Win the Lottery*
and *Wealth Without Wall Street*

**Check out Don McNay's *Life Lessons from the Lottery:
Protecting Your Money in a Scary World* and keep an
eye out for future titles in the *Life Lessons* series.**

CPSIA information can be obtained at www.ICGtesting.com
Printed in the USA
LVOW050512210313

325351LV00002B/165/P